House
:: OF ::
CARDS

HOUSE OF CARDS

Sarah Hamilton

PAVILION

CONTENTS

PROJECTS

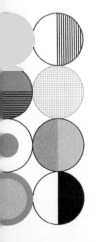

WELCOME!

CELEBRATE THE VERY BEST IN *contemporary* GREETING CARD DESIGN. **MEET THE MAKERS** IN THEIR STUDIOS AS THEY REVEAL **THEIR INSPIRATIONS** AND SHARE THEIR IDEAS. EXPLORE **NEW TECHNIQUES** **AND DISCOVER HOW TO** *make money* FROM YOUR CREATIONS.

Each card is a work of art, the perfect way to discover and explore creative techniques through the guidance and skill of ten exciting artists.

INTRODUCTION

Artists are, by their very nature, collectors. We surround ourselves with treasures to inspire us in our day-to-day work. Pebbles, leaves and seed heads wrestle for shelf space in my studio, yet greetings cards collected on my travels take pride of place. I've long been addicted to making and collecting cards, since first handprinting them on my kitchen table in the nineties to help make ends meet after art college, and I am not alone. In *House of Cards*, nine fellow artists join me to share our passion for card-making to get you started on your own creative journey.

This practical and insightful book offers a wealth of creative tips, with ten visually exciting projects and a fascinating history and context of cards. In addition, industry professionals offer practical advice to help you to maximise sales of your own handmade cards, or to work with art publishers to license your designs.

We invite you to join the creative fun by exploring these easy-to-follow, step-by-step projects, which introduce many different techniques, from silkscreen printing to stitching. Roll up your sleeves and dive straight in: much of what you need is inexpensive and easily accessible. Whilst we guide you through the projects you'll discover that, with thought and imagination, cards become artworks in their own right. As your confidence and skill levels grow we encourage you to experiment with your own designs, referring to the Finding Inspiration chapter as you go.

There is much more to cards than beautiful pictures, as you'll discover in our chapters A Brief History and Charity Cards. Card sales help fund galleries, museums, charities, shops and, of course, artists and designers. Their wider cultural impact was brought home to me when I read the words, 'If everyone who'd complimented our beautiful gallery had bought "just a card" we'd still be open', from shopkeepers who'd recently had to close down. This poignant observation reminds us how significant revenue generated by small sales is to so many, and led to my starting the 'Just a Card' campaign to highlight the value of each and every sale.

I hope this book will inspire you to embrace the joyful world of card-making and sharing. Your friends and family will certainly delight in receiving your cards as much as you enjoy making them.

Sarah Hamilton

A BRIEF HISTORY

JAKKI BROWN

Jakki Brown is co-owner and editor of *Progressive Greetings Worldwide*, the only monthly greeting card business-to-business magazine in the world. Currently also joint general secretary of the UK's Greeting Card Association, she has had a ringside seat in the greeting card industry for over 25 years. Here, she shares her passion for and knowledge of the history of card giving.

We live in a technological age. Our email inboxes overflow, incessant 'pings' punctuate our days to fanfare the arrival of text messages on our mobile phones, and our Facebook 'likes' tally and trending on Twitter are virtual popularity contests. Communicating via email or text messages are effective means for information dissemination, but I doubt they will ever feel as good as receiving an actual greeting card that has been specially selected for us, that we can hold in our hand and which contains a personal message that we can keep forever. After all, you can't put an email on the mantelpiece. This book is a celebration of a very special, ever-evolving and, most importantly, tangible social communication medium – the greeting card.

Greeting cards are popular all over the globe and especially so in the USA, Australia and the UK. Australia is the third largest market for greeting cards per capita with 22 cards bought per person each year. In the USA, the annual retail sales of cards is estimated to be somewhere in the region of $7.5 billion, and the two largest producers of cards, Hallmark Cards and American Greetings, are based there. But it is in the UK that more cards are sent per head of population than any other

nation. Leading from the top, Queen Elizabeth II will dispatch 46,000 cards this year to centenarians and couples marking their high wedding anniversaries, and Her Majesty received over 70,000 cards to mark her 90th birthday from members of her public filled with their good wishes. The UK market supports over 400 greeting card publishers, ranging from huge multi-nationals to small self-publishing artists, and almost two billion cards are bought annually.

So where did this love of sending and receiving greeting cards all start from? It is not a modern phenomenon. The ancient Chinese exchanged messages of goodwill to celebrate New Year, and handmade paper valentines were given and received in many parts of Europe from around the beginning of the 15th century. In fact, valentines cards were the first greeting cards to be produced commercially at the start of the 19th century. The early valentines cards are as varied in style and tone as their modern-day counterparts, ranging from the elaborately sentimental to the crudely humorous. But it was Esther Howland, daughter of a large book and stationery store owner from Worcester, Massachusetts, USA, who produced the first mass-produced valentines, confections of elaborately embossed paper lace, in 1847.

The first commercially produced Christmas card predates Esther Howland's valentines by a few years. It was the bright idea of the eminent Victorian, Sir Henry Cole, who later went on to organise the UK's Great Exhibition of 1851 and to become the first director of London's Victoria & Albert Museum in 1852. In 1843, finding himself too busy to write the customary Christmas-time letters to his friends and family, Sir Henry commissioned the artist Sir John Callcott Horsley to create an image that could be lithographed and hand-coloured. A thousand of these cards

Very few of the first commercially produced Christmas card, conceived and commissioned by Sir Henry Cole, are in existence today. As well as depicting good deeds, the feeding and the clothing of the poor, the design showed a family enjoying Christmas festivities with glasses of wine. This upset members of the Temperance movement who destroyed many of the cards.

The robin has been a popular subject on British Christmas cards ever since Victorian times when postmen wore red jackets. This linocut print card was designed by Sam Marshall (see pages 58–67 for more about her work).

were produced, printed on stiff pasteboard, and those not required by Sir Henry for his personal use were put on sale for one shilling each in a retail emporium, Summerly's Home Treasurer in London's Old Bond Street, run by Cole's business partner Joseph Cundall.

Sir Henry Cole's 'invention' was not an immediate success and the tradition of sending Christmas cards did not really become established until the 1860s following the introduction of the Penny Post, when cheaper printing techniques became more widespread, bringing down the cost of such cards. Today, the UK's Greeting Card Association's annual industry awards, the Henries, are named in recognition of Sir Henry Cole's contribution. In the USA, the LOUIEs are awarded in the International Greeting Cards Award Competition, and these are named after Louis Prang, the German-born Boston lithographer, often referred to as the 'father of the American Christmas card', who began selling Christmas cards there in the mid 1870s.

Holly and mistletoe, Christmas trees, winter scenes and Father Christmas (in his various guises) all took their place on Victorian mantelpieces. Pigs were also popular as the Victorians thought they were hilarious. Once the tradition of sending cards at Christmas was established, Easter cards came along next. Initially, these featured designs using only purple and silver, the ecclesiastical colours, but it wasn't long before fluffy chicks and spring flowers made an appearance.

Greeting cards are there to chronicle our lives, marking our first breath to our last, giving people the opportunity to tell others that they care with a handwritten message inside what is, after all, a work of art.

As the years rolled on, so the creating and sending of greeting cards increased and their value cherished. Even during the paper shortages of the Second World War, Christmas cards continued to be produced as they were recognised as crucial to morale. This continues to be the case, borne out by a recent study by Mindlab International, an independent scientific research organisation, the results of which showed that people had a much greater emotional response to receiving handwritten cards than to emails, texts and social media messages.

The purchase of a greeting card is one of the most complicated buying decisions. One of the few products always bought for someone else, the selection is overlaid with the purchaser's self-image/ego, and this is the reason why there is a place for such diversity of styles.

The sending and giving of greeting cards is just as relevant today as it has ever been. As I write this, my office is piled high with boxes, packages and envelopes full of greeting cards, all of which are being entered into this year's Henries awards by hundreds of card publishers and designers. We had 14,000 entries last year, tangible proof that greeting cards are as popular as ever.

FINDING INSPIRATION

SARAH HAMILTON

Every artistic discipline, from fine art to photography, from ceramics to sculpture, is a delicate balance between the artist's personal influences and his or her favoured technical methods.

This book celebrates the imagination, originality and skills of artists who make cards. The finished projects may seem effortless, yet in reality many hours have been spent drawing, researching, practising, investigating and experimenting along the way. In ten information-packed chapters, these artists will reveal how they arrived at their finished creations from both a practical and a creative perspective, as the concepts are as interesting and diverse as the techniques they have used.

Many books present step-by-step projects for you to copy, yet very few offer you the chance to develop your own fresh ideas and turn them into personal designs, a process that is extremely rewarding. In this chapter my fellow contributors and I share with you techniques and thought processes that motivate and inspire us, to encourage you to develop your own distinctive interests as you explore your creative versatility.

My own designs have been described as 'deceptively simple', which is very gratifying as the beholders of my work have appreciated the 'behind the scenes' processes that make up my imagery. Every aspect is considered. Endless colour combinations are explored. Paper is tested and retested for texture and absorbency. Shapes are carefully judged, as the amount of colour affects the overall look. If this appears seamless then I'm delighted. I adore creative freedom but ultimately the juxtapositions of scale, material, colour and texture make or break a design.

It has taken considerable time to develop my working process and, of course, I'm not always happy with the results. However, it's satisfying to have developed a visual language that I can use to work through my ideas. It takes patience and confidence to develop a way of working and no-one can teach you how to respond to the world, but I'd like to explore some ways that will help you to clarify your personal interests. Discover what genuinely inspires you and you'll be able to develop a way of working that leads you to projects that tell your own story.

I was asked recently what I was most proud of about my work and without hesitation it is this: that it is instantly recognisable as mine. I was happiest as a teacher when I felt the end result of a student's work was a piece of art that most successfully represented his or her personality. Being able to express ourselves is one of the greatest gifts we can have.

REPEATED PATTERNS IN
nature
A PASSION FOR COLOUR AND
TEXTURE
AN EMOTIVE RESPONSE TO THE
landscape
memories of a
SPECIAL PLACE

a JOURNEY OF discovery

1 KEEP SKETCHBOOKS Record your thoughts and ideas in your visual diary – personal and private if you wish. Have one on you at all times – you never know when inspiration will strike. Vary your materials – crayons, paint, ink, pencils. Stick pages in. Tear pages out. Make a mess. The more relaxed you are, the livelier your designs will be.

2 Become a collector

Pebbles, acorns, leaves, seaweed – fragments of nature foraged on country walks, or beachcombed flotsam and jestsam, these are the artist's jewels. Fill your pockets with discarded oddities – shards of rusty tin or driftwood for texture, sea glass for colour. You'll discover a wealth of textures, colours and forms if you surround yourself with these everyday objects of desire.

3 DRAW Take your pencil and try to capture the spirit of an object. Drawing is a journey of discovery – there's so much more to an object than your perceived memory of it. If you focus on appreciating the thing before you rather than on making a technically proficient rendition of it, you'll appreciate colours, textures and oddities to extend your visual vocabulary.

I recently spent an entire day sketching poppy seed heads plucked from my garden. A day spent examining every nuance filled me with new ideas for shapes, textures and composition.

Sarah Hamilton

4 *Explore positive and negative spaces*

There's so much more to a shape than its edges. Consider where your images are placed on your paper and how much of an object is to be hidden or shown. Imagine, for example, an image with a leaf in the centre, and then the next one with a quarter of the same leaf, and another with a picture of a leaf at a very different angle.

5 EMBRACE ALL YOUR SENSES

Sound, smell, touch and taste are as evocative as sight when producing or appreciating visual art. Heady sweet-smelling honeysuckle on a summer's day, the texture of lichen or seed heads, the dulcet tones of a favourite song, all these can be as inspiring as any gallery artwork.

6 BEFRIEND YOUR COMPUTER

The relationship between artist and computer is sometimes uncomfortable; some see computer art as less tactile than traditional techniques. Pixel-generated images can appear soul-less, while a hand-drawn image is full of life and expression. However, a computer is a wonderful tool to help you to increase your visual vocabulary, so do use it to experiment with scale, composition and colour.

> Much of my work begins with text, with poetry and stories, snippets of which find their way into my books and papercuts.
>
> *Sarah Morpeth*

> I keep going back to my sketchbooks even years after having completed them as I always find them to be a source of inspiration – and sometimes surprises and insights.
>
> *Gabriela Szulman*

SELLING CARDS

We asked the talented artists who have created the card projects for this book to share some of their top tips to help you to maximise your sales when selling your cards commercially.

> When creating artwork I ask myself, 'Who will be the person buying this card?' My aim is to bring joy to that person when they see what I have created.
>
> *Lynn Giunta*

Gabriela Szulman adds a collage 'signature' to the back of one of her collage cards.

1 *Make the card to fit the envelope*

It's a good idea to make your cards to fit neatly inside standard envelope sizes as this can really help to keep your costs down. A finished card measuring 10.5cm wide by 15cm high, for example, fits perfectly into a C5 envelope. If your cards are going to be non-standard sizes, research the availability and cost of envelopes first.

2 CHOOSE YOUR ENVELOPE TO ENHANCE YOUR CARD

Envelope choice is very important as it frames the card on the shop shelf, so choose wisely and don't skimp on quality. A brightly coloured envelope can really make a card pop, especially if the card itself has a white background.

3 *Test the market for your card designs*

Before you make large quantities of your card designs, try selling them at a local craft market. You will discover not only which motifs are most popular but also what other card occasions people would like to buy from you.

4 DON'T FORGET THE BACK STORY

Continue your design onto the back of the card: create a logo and remember to include your contact details (website/contact number or email). This is free publicity and it gives people an opportunity to find out more about you and your work.

5 TO BAG OR NOT TO BAG

Many cards sold in shops are supplied cellophane wrapped. Check with the retail outlet that you would like to sell to if this is a necessary requirement for them. There are cellophane bags made to fit most standard card and envelope sizes. Remember, products that do not conform to standard sizes will cost more to manufacture and you may also have to make a minimum order, and this can be an unnecessary drain on your precious starting-out finances.

6 RESEARCH CARD PRICING

Take time to analyse the pricing of cards already in the market before setting the price of your card designs, looking at cards that are similar to yours in size, style and quality. Cards with a finish, such as gold foil, for example, will cost more, so be careful to compare like with like or you may be in danger of overcharging. You need to balance making your profit margins whilst charging a price that enables a retailer to make theirs.

7 *Consider the needs of your market*

Some territories may have specific needs that you may have to make allowances for when designing cards for that market. For example, cards smaller than 12cm by 17cm are often deemed too small by Australian retailers, while in the United States square cards cost more to post.

8 CREATE A COHESIVE CARD COLLECTION

Aim to design a collection of cards rather than random designs that may or may not go well together.

So often, customers pick up a card and immediately turn it over. Consider the packaging, the graphics for your name and website, and the sticker on the bag fold, as all combine to make the finished work.

Sarah Hamilton

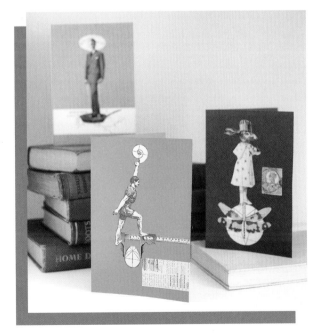

It is a good idea to develop a range that is unified in terms of look, technique, materials and sizes as Gabriela Szulman has done here with this collection of her collage cards.

LICENSING DESIGNS

JEHANE BODEN SPIERS

Many artists make, distribute and sell cards themselves, through their websites or at art shows or design events. Another option that is open to them is to choose an art publisher to handle the production and sale of their designs. One company specialising in representing artists to publishers is Yellow House Art Licensing. Co-owner Jehane Boden Spiers shares how this process works for both artist and agent.

I've always been fascinated by the impact certain images have on our visual world. Inspired by the conversations around the creative process and the insights into how different artworks were received, I made the decision to move from designer to art agent, co-founding Yellow House Art Licensing with illustration agent Sue Bateman in 2011.

Art licensing is the process whereby an artist, agent or third party grants the reproduction rights for a specific image, on a specific product, for an agreed period of time, for sale within a given territory. Let's say, as an example, on greeting cards, for a three-year term, for sale in the UK only – this scenario allows the option to license the same design for the same product in a different territory.

Licensing an image doesn't stop the artist from selling the physical original artwork: the artwork belongs to the artist whether the image has been part-licensed or the full copyright sold, and so he or she is free to sell it. However, if the artist wants to license an image after selling the original artwork, it is crucial that they have access to a high-resolution file of it. Unless the full copyright has been sold, the copyright in, and therefore rights to license, the image remain with the artist (or the artist's estate) until a fixed number of years after the artist's death –

70 years in the UK, for example, although the length of time may vary in different countries. If full copyright has been sold, then the artist no longer has the rights to license the image.

It's a thrill for artists to see their work licensed as a greeting card or, indeed, any product. As well as being a clear endorsement of their creative efforts, it can provide an important source of income. There are three ways payment can be made: flat-fee (a one-off payment), royalty only (earning a percentage on net receipts), or an advance against royalties (a payment earned off at an agreed percentage before royalty payments begin).

When an artist's artwork is licensed as a greeting card, it acts as a very successful calling card. The first thing we do when we receive a card is to look at the back where a credit to the artist is included, often with a photograph or statement about their work. Yellow House artists have often found that they have been directly commissioned to create original artwork as a result of their images being on cards.

Interestingly, securing a licensed greeting card range can also be a crucial stepping-stone to attracting other licensees who look to the greeting card industry to see which new trends or artists are selling well. They often use this knowledge as the basis for making decisions on those images to license for their own product areas, for example, tins and trays, stationery, textiles and homewares.

Successful greeting card ranges can expand to include over 60 or even 100 designs generating a very healthy income for the artist, especially if they are royalty-linked. Card companies will run profitable ranges for years, whilst other product designs might only have a shelf life of a couple of years. Yellow House's first card licence, 'Copper Tree' by Janine Partington (licensed to the Almanac Gallery), has been running now for over five years, and it is stocked in outlets across the world, from the UK to Australia.

As an art agency, the most important decision for us when selecting artists to represent is to know that we will be able to talk about their work with excitement and enthusiasm. Their artwork needs to be consistent in quality and to have its own uniquely identifiable personality, different from any artist we already represent. If we can see a fit with the needs of our existing clients, we'll meet with the artist personally to discuss the possibility of signing them as a new artist. A close working relationship with our artists is key, and we aim to offer creative direction and feedback whilst respecting their artistic vision.

All the images on these two pages, from artists represented by Yellow House Art Licensing, have been licensed onto greeting cards. They are, opposite from top to bottom, Snowy Tree © Cressida Bell and Musicat © Paul Thurlby; and above, from top to bottom, The Meeting © Janine Partington, Cat © Nancy Nicholson and Christmas Damask © Jehane Boden Spiers.

My personal view of our role as agents is that we are here to complement the artistic process, creating a dialogue about an artist's work, and finding the right partners to publish his or her work. Whether it be as a range of greeting cards or a series of children's books, a set of tableware or a collection of open-edition prints, we are looking to find opportunities that suit the individual style of the artist and strengthens brand awareness.

Exhibiting at trade fairs is a key part of our promotional calendar and we have working relationships with partner agents in Spain, Japan and the USA. We advertise in trade press and write regular features for these publications as well as guest blogs. We are very active on social media and try to share as much of an artist's content as we can.

We aim to create a positive, enjoyable and long-term working relationship with each artist and every client. We welcome submissions from both established and new artists – illustrators, printmakers and craftspeople.

REPRESENTING YOURSELF: JESSICA HOGARTH

As well as designing her own range of products, which is mainly focused around colourful greeting cards available in shops and galleries across the UK, artist Jessica Hogarth has a growing portfolio of prints and patterns that are available to license directly from her own website (jessicahogarth.com). She also works on collaborations and commissions for a variety of companies and individuals to produce a wide range of surface pattern design repeats and placement prints. Here she shares her experiences of representing herself and her work:

'The freelance illustration side of my business allows me to create work for multiple product areas, such as outdoor furniture, fashion apparel and kitchen products. I am either commissioned to create a piece of work, or I license my existing artwork, allowing me to retain copyright and continue to utilise it either for my own products, or to offer it to other clients for different product areas. This is both an exciting and lucrative side of my business; it is great to see my work on products that I cannot afford to manufacture myself, as well as providing a welcome boost to my income as an artist.

I exhibit at a number of trade shows each year, both in the UK and overseas, where I meet wholesale buyers for my products. As a result, my products are currently stocked in a number of high-street outlets and many independent retailers in the UK, as well as being distributed across several overseas territories.'

Jessica's Snowy Days Ice Skaters card, left, was licensed by Deva Designs for a Christmas giftwrap range, below.

CHARITY CARDS

DAVID OAKES

Charity cards are as much part of Christmas as turkeys and Santa, and artists work on the designs months in advance. For some, designing a multitude of Christmas cards is a full-time job;others, such as British artist and actor David Oakes, create a specific image in support of their chosen charity. David, who was commissioned by the British Lung Foundation to design a card, shares some insights into this collaboration, and highlights how the deceptively humble card can have a huge positive effect on people's lives.

A wide range of charities the world over produce and sell millions of greeting cards each year. These cards raise the profile of the charities, inform people about their work, and are often as much about tradition and goodwill as they are about fundraising. As one medium-sized UK charity that I spoke to told me: 'We roughly bring in around £15,000 to £20,000 per year through Christmas card sales. Our total income is about £6 million per year, so card sales play a relatively small part, but they provide an opportunity for our supporters to help us and to get something in return.'

For many charities, however, the revenue generated by greeting card sales is vital to enable them to continue their valuable work, and they manufacture cards all year round, not just at Christmas. One such not-for-profit organisation is ARTHOUSE Meath, a social enterprise presenting the skills and talents of people living with severe epilepsy, learning and physical difficulties. Over 70 ARTHOUSE Meath artists, some dealing with brain injuries, physical disabilities or impaired sight and memory, collaborate with professional art instructors to create saleable artwork. These sessions yield a treasure trove of inspired designs, including cards for every occasion, and 100 per cent of the sales revenue goes towards sustaining the enterprise, helping it to grow and evolve.

Charities put considerable effort and energy into selecting images to reflect their aims and objectives, as well as generating maximum revenue and media exposure. Artists are often chosen well in advance and carefully briefed. My commission to design a Christmas card by the British Lung Foundation (BLF), whose aim is to improve care, prevent, treat and cure lung diseases, was months in discussion, well ahead even of the Christmas preceding the one for which my design was requested. My brief was that the design should be fun and creative, in keeping with the positive outlook the BLF and its staff have on life. I was provided with the freedom to not only use my preferred medium, but also my chosen dimensions for the card. Our discussions led to my pencil drawing of a reindeer displaying BLF's distinctive red colour as, 'It's Christmas – we'd like it to include some colour to bring it to life on our supporters' mantelpieces.'

The sending of Christmas cards continues to be a very popular tradition and for many it is important to support charities at a time of goodwill and sharing. Charity cards are a tangible reminder of the 'behind the scenes' work so many people do all year long. Often a charity card is our first introduction to a specific cause giving charities an opportunity to spread their message during the festive season and beyond.

Opposite The final version of the Christmas card created by David Oakes for the British Lung Foundation.

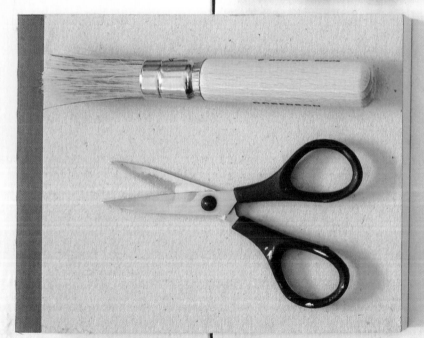

BASIC TOOL KIT

In each chapter the featured artist has provided guidance on the tools required for their chosen technique, as well as a specific materials list for the card they have made. Listed here are basic items you may also find useful as you explore card-making.

Graphite pencils Test various hard or soft leads for different uses – soft leads for sketching, harder leads for graphic work.

Light box These are available in several sizes and the smaller ones are relatively inexpensive.

Bone folder A creasing and scoring tool for clean crisp folds, very important when using heavyweight paper prone to wrinkling.

Metal ruler A solid metal ruler – the heavier the better – is very useful for tearing or cutting paper.

Guillotine When purchasing, look out for features such as changeable blades, and for special settings that enable you to score or to cut rounded corners, for example.

Scissors It's worth spending a little extra on these to equip yourself with quality, and invest in a few different-sized pairs.

Rotary cutter Experiment with different shaped cutting blades.

Cellophane bags There is a wide range of clear display bags available, with or without a self-seal strip (if you choose without, you can add your own personalised sticker). Shop around and request samples; consider weight, texture, static, as well as price.

Baker's twine and string Ideal for making card bundles.

Paper and envelopes Experiment with the sheer breadth of textures, weights and colours available, and always use the best quality you can afford. Read Silvie Turner's *The Book of Fine Paper* for a celebration and explanation of the world of artist's paper.

Other useful tools Eraser, scalpel, compass, coloured pencils, various adhesives including a PVA glue-stick, adhesive tape (double-sided and clear), masking tape, ruler, paint brushes, spray mount, hole punch, scalpel, craft knife and cutting mat.

PROJECTS

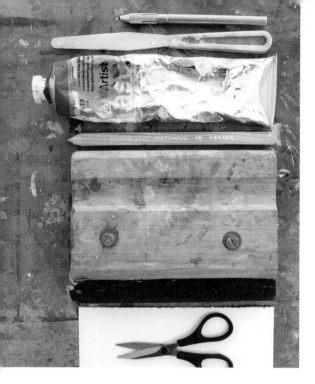

I am a London-based artist with a passion for colour and drawing. I make cards, prints, woodblocks and homewares from a studio in my mid-century modern home. Views over the woods towards the city beyond inspire my designs, which all begin as sketchbook drawings. After studying fine art and printmaking at Central St Martins, I began by making cards that successfully sold in many design-led stores, enabling me to develop my studio and broaden my commissions.

SARAH HAMILTON

Silkscreen printing is my first love – lifting a screen to reveal a hit of rich colour is heaven. Essentially, screen-printing is a printmaking process where ink is forced through a fine mesh using a squeegee. Areas of the screen blocked by a paper or photographic stencil and masking fluid will remain the hue of the paper or fabric below. A relatively straightforward process, it does take some experimenting with colour overlays to fully appreciate its creative potential.

Cards have always been central to my work. They are a great way to experiment with colour and design combinations, and to gauge responses to new images. People are surprised that I still make my cards in my studio, but for me there is joy in the texture and tone of the paper and in ensuring that each card is perfectly printed and packaged. My cards often lead people to my other work and I'm told clients collect and frame them.

Every mirror, print, card and woodblock made in my sunny south London studio reflects my passion for colour, drawing and textured materials. Joyful, fresh and contemporary, with a mid-century modern Scandinavian feel, my images emerge from sketchbooks and are hand or digitally printed. Colours and their effect on each other fascinate me. Put simply, my colours must sing and so my studio creaks under the weight of endless shade tests and samples.

TOOLS AND TECHNIQUES

When I first met a silkscreen press about 30 years ago, it was love at first sight. There is a misconception that bulky, expensive equipment is needed for silkscreen printing when, in reality, a simple, efficient press can be bought or constructed inexpensively. I've made hundreds of commissions on a printing press I made when I left college and it fits neatly under my plan chest when not in use.

Silkscreen printing is like cooking with colour. Many of the tools in my studio originate from the kitchen – spatulas, mixing bowls, a blender, apron. A splash of red here, a dollop of pink there, the combinations are endless. Mixing pots of pure colour and printing with a variety of opacities means you can never entirely predict results. I always get excited when I lift a screen to discover the print below – some look great, while others head straight to the bin.

Screen-printing ink is made by mixing acrylic colours with a base medium, a clear screen-printing paste. There are a number of available brands – I use Lascaux. There is no prescribed ratio for the mix: this is a matter of personal preference and experimentation depending on how opaque you want your ink to be. As a broad guide, a deep colour is achieved by an approximate 1:1 ratio; if you prefer more transparent inks, then add less neat colour to the paste. For the Bird and Oak Leaf card, I printed the first print layer using a deep colour and a more transparent ink for the second print layer, which allows for a third colour to be created where the second colour overlays the first.

Silkscreen printing is great for making multiple cards, so if you'd like to continue making a number of cards, keep printing until you've reached your desired amount. Roughly five tablespoons of silkscreen paste mixed with your preferred colour density will make sufficient ink to print a good run. Do ensure your first colour is fully dry before you print the second colour.

A corner of my studio with a couple of my sketchbooks and a work-in-progress wall full of my designs.

MY INSPIRATIONS

So many things influence me from artists including Milton Avery, William Scott, Paul Klee and Georges Braque, to architects such as Frank Lloyd Wright and Finn Juhl. I gravitate towards art, architecture and design that is clean, fresh and deceptively simple. I'm a big reader and I especially enjoy books with strong visual emphasis – striking landscapes or details of place or nature, for example.

I adore fifties textile and poster designs for their sophisticated, yet deceptively effortless, beauty. Folk art from North America and Mexican papercuts and tinwork also influence my work. I often draw from objects picked up on my travels to Japan, Scandinavia, Africa, Mexico and Sri Lanka. I am inspired by the quintessentially British aesthetic of artists including Eric Ravilious, Eric Gill and Edward Bawden, whose art has a delicate yet timeless quality.

Any leftover prepared ink can be stored and reused if kept in an airtight jar.

bird AND O A K *leaf*

Silkscreen Print

PAPER FOR SKETCHING • RULER • PENCILS • TRACING PAPER • NEWSPRINT PAPER• SCISSORS • A4 SHEETS OF ARTIST'S PAPER • SCREEN-PRINTING MASKING FLUID OR MASKING TAPE • ARTIST'S ACRYLIC PAINT IN TWO COLOURS • SCREEN-PRINTING PASTE • MIXING BOWL FOR MIXING THE SCREEN-PRINTING INKS • JAM JARS WITH AIRTIGHT LIDS FOR STORING UNUSED MIXED INKS • PALETTE KNIFE • SILKSCREEN FRAME • BASIC PRESS • SQUEEGEE • CLEANING CLOTHS • SCALPEL • METAL RULER • CUTTING MAT

Cutting paper is the least complex way of making screen-printing stencils, yet can produce striking results. Simple bold shapes work well, as can be seen in this Bird and Oak Leaf card design. Experimenting with the ink opacity and printing with just two colours creates a third overlapping colour. The subtly drawn edges of the oak leaf contrast with the bolder form of the bird, and the success of the end result depends on this juxtaposition of shape and colour.

1 Draw a 15cm square on a sheet of paper. This will be your printed area. Draw your card design onto the paper within the confines of the box.

2 Trace your card design onto a small sheet of tracing paper.

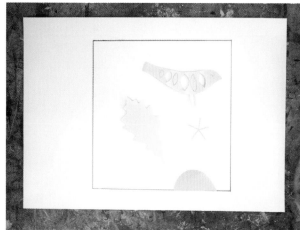

3 Transfer your design onto newsprint paper using the traced image. Cut out each individual shape to make your paper printing stencils.

4 Draw a second 15cm template box on one of the sheets of A4 paper you will print on. Place the cut stencils for the first colour (orange in this case) in position relating to your design. You may need a few practice runs using simple stencils to work out the two colour positions.

5 Use water-resistant plastic parcel tape or silkscreen masking fluid (as I have used here – please note it is also orange) to mask off a 15cm square on your screen. Place your A4 drawn paper template box beneath the printing square. When these are perfectly aligned, tape two small pieces of paper to your print bed base (not the paper) to mark the two edges of the paper. You will use these as a guide as you continue printing to ensure your A4 paper is placed accurately when printing further colours. Mix your two silkscreen printing ink colours by combining your chosen acrylic colours with the screen-printing paste (see Tools and Techniques for more advice).

6 Now you are ready to apply ink and print. The process is described in detail in steps 7–10 where the second colour, pink in this case, is being applied. The photograph, right, shows how the print will look after printing with the first ink colour (orange). The first print stencils have been removed and the second print stencils have been placed in position, to mask off those areas that will not be printed on the second ink printing. After each colour is printed, you must clean the ink from the silkscreen frame before applying further colours. (Do not allow the ink to dry on the mesh as this will block it and render it unusable.) Always ensure your first colour is dry before you print your next colour.

7 Lay your screen down. Use a palette knife to scoop a line of ink below your 15cm box, slightly wider than it. Prop up the edge of the screen using pieces of cardboard/wood. This creates a gap of approximately 1cm between the screen and the print bed base when printing, to ensure the screen doesn't stick to the paper and smudge.

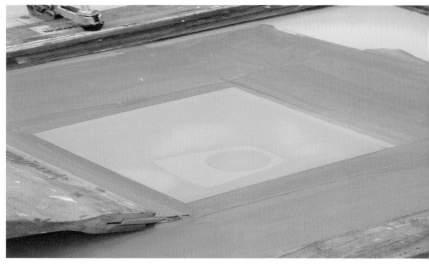

8 Holding the squeegee at a 45-degree angle and lifting the screen slightly higher, 'flood' the screen with ink by pushing it to the back of the screen. At this stage the screen should not be touching the paper – you're not printing, you're simply preparing the ink ahead of printing as the screen needs to be full of ink in order to achieve a consistent coverage.

9 Now to print. Lower the screen. Pull the ink over the boxed area, pressing down firmly and holding the squeegee at a 45-degree angle. The wet ink will hold the stencils in place ready for your next print pull.

10 Lift up the screen, remove the stencils and admire your work – always the best bit! If you're not happy with anything at either the first or second printing, try again on a new piece of paper.

OPPOSITE My prints are primarily about exploring colour relationships, with deceptively simple contrasting forms and textures. A combination of traditional screen-printing techniques and digital printing allows me to be both experimental and exacting in my design work.

11 The finished design once both the first and the second ink colours have been printed. A third colour (deep orange) is created where the pink overlays the un-masked areas of the orange.

12 Trim and fold your cards. My finished card is 22cm x 15cm after trimming, 11cm x 15cm after folding. The printed design will partially wrap round the back of the card, leaving a strip of white to add your designer details to.

I grew up in a family where making things was always encouraged – I have many happy memories of rooting through drawers of sequins and beads, sewing and gluing, and spending hours imagining what I could create. I took a class in college that introduced me to hand lettering, which eventually led to a degree in graphic design. As an artist in the visual studios at Hallmark Cards in Kansas City, Missouri, I spend each and every working day creating with talented and inspiring people.

LYNN GIUNTA

I love to design with cut paper – it reminds me of being a kid and doing craft projects at the kitchen table. There is nothing more satisfying to me than sitting down with scissors and an array of coloured papers to create a card. Decoupage (from the French word *découper* meaning to cut out) is the art of decorating a surface with paper cutouts or illustrations. It is a technique more often used on three-dimensional objects including furniture, but I like to make two-dimensional cards this way. It is magical how compositions come to life as I start to cut. Quite often the negative shapes that I threw into the scrap pile end up being what I use.

Designing cards is what I do professionally and has been since I stepped out of college over 30 years ago. Whether creating with brush and ink or scissors and paper, I love developing card collections for publication. Positive words, cut paper shapes and beautiful colour palettes are central to my work, and I aim to keep my designs simple to speak to the child at the heart of each of us. My most successful designs are simple and impactful; I think the real trick is to know when to stop and let the artwork be.

Being creative is a part of everything I do – from making gifts or learning a new craft to creating in my studio at home. No matter where I am working, I surround myself with inspiration – I believe that continually looking at good design helps me to figure out who I am as a designer. Some of it is work that I have done, some of it is from friends or research off the Internet – but it reminds me of how much I love to create. I look around at my colourful collection and get excited about starting on the next project.

TOOLS AND TECHNIQUES

For the craft of decoupage you will need to collect together a range of different papers. The weight of the paper is important: tissue paper works well because it is thin and transparent but you can utilise just about any regular-weight paper (it is best to avoid very heavy paper as it will not stay glued down). Do experiment with patterned paper as well as solid colours. You'll find that the transparency of tissue paper allows for unexpected surprises when colours overlap, but don't be tempted to put down too many layers or it will start to get muddy.

I use scissors for cutting out, but you may also find that a craft knife comes in useful. You'll also need Mod Podge or matte medium (to use as glue), a brush and a piece of board to glue your design onto. It must be thick enough to handle many layers of the wet glaze otherwise it will buckle and warp, and it must be white because the tissue papers are transparent. I've used a heavyweight (No. 100) Crescent cold press illustration board. If the surface of your board isn't white, you can paint it with white acrylic or gesso.

When designing a new card, typically I will start out doing rough sketches of what I'm thinking might be a good idea; I sketch onto tracing paper so that I can overlap and redraw as I work out my idea.

Sometimes I work through many layers of tracing paper, sketching and redrawing and changing the hierarchy of my design.

MY INSPIRATIONS

A few of the artists that really inspire me are Corita Kent, Paul Rand and Alexander Girard. I also belong to a lunchtime sketch group that has really motivated me to try new things and to create something every day.

I use my sketchbook to try to push myself out of my creative comfort zone, although the major themes you'll find there are generally the same: brush lettering, images that make me happy, positive words, cut paper shapes and letters, painted patterns and experimental colour combinations.

My sketchbooks help me see where I've been and where I am going.

FRUIT Bowl

Decoupage

WHITE HEAVYWEIGHT BOARD• SCISSORS • PAPER • PENCIL • TRACING PAPER • PLAIN AND PATTERNED TISSUE PAPERS • OTHER PAPERS (I USED A BROWN PAPER BAG AND GRAPH PAPER) • CAMERA • MOD PODGE OR OTHER MATTE OR GLOSS MEDIUM • SMALL PLASTIC CUP • NEWSPRINT PAPER • BRUSH • • PAPER TOWELS • CARDSTOCK • DOUBLE-SIDED TAPE

For my Fruit Bowl decoupage card I used not only tissue paper but brown paper and graph paper too. For my fruits I decided on an apple and a pear, which are nice basic shapes, and cutting the apple open made it much more interesting. Your choice of shapes and tissue colours will make this project uniquely yours. Be willing to let happy accidents happen once you start to glue your design down – the fun is in discovering something that you hadn't planned to do.

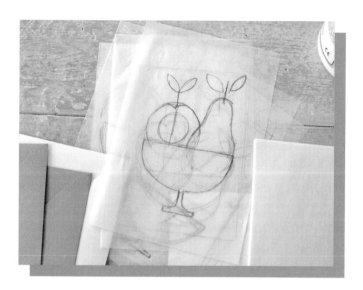

1 Trim a piece of white heavyweight board to fit into a standard sized envelope (mine is 13cm x 18cm). Sketch out your design on a piece of tracing paper cut to the same size to give you a pattern to follow.

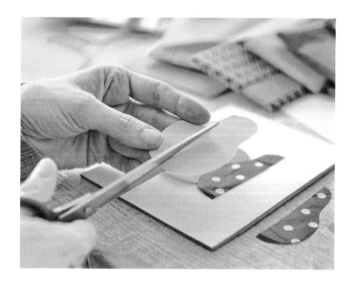

2 Cut out your fruit shapes. I cut out two pear shapes, one patterned and one solid, then cut both roughly in half, which I overlapped to make the finished pear shape, saving the leftover halves for other projects.

3 Take the apple shape and cut a round hole in the middle. Cut out semicircles of tissue paper in different colours; these should be large enough to cover the hole and overlap it and each other.

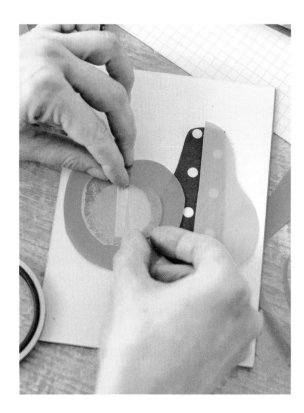

4 Finish cutting the other pieces you will need: for the bowl, I used a brown paper bag, adding strips of grey paper for decoration; for the tablecloth, I used graph paper; and for the stems, leaves and seeds, I used a variety of solid and patterned tissue papers. Experiment with colours and composition.

5 Once you are happy with your design, it is time to glue it down. Pour a small amount of Mod Podge (or matte/gloss medium) into a small plastic cup. Clear away all the paper scraps and lay down some newsprint paper beneath your board to keep your work surface clean. I often take a quick reference photo to help me remember how I had pieces positioned once I start gluing, although I don't follow it exactly.

6 Carefully move your pieces off the board onto a spare sheet of paper. You will start by gluing the pieces on the bottom layer, working your way up to the top layer. For the design pictured, the order of gluing is graph paper tablecloth first, then the fruit shapes (pear then apple), and finally the bowl.

7 Paint a layer of the glaze onto the board where you intend to place your first shape, in this case the graph paper tablecloth. Carefully place your piece of paper onto the wet area, working from one edge to the other, and then paint a layer of glaze on top (the glaze goes on white but will dry clear). Use your fingers to gently push out wrinkles – it's messy so keep paper towels handy. It's really hard to pick up a piece once it has been placed as the paper will often tear. Leave it where it is and move on. It doesn't need to be perfect.

8 Next add the half pieces of the pear. Paint a layer of glaze where you want to position the first half of the pear, place the paper and paint glaze on top, then repeat the process with the other half overlapping it where it joins the first piece. Use your fingers to smooth out the pieces.

9 Paint a layer of glaze where the apple shape is to be positioned. Place the apple, brush more glaze on top, and then place first one middle piece and then the other, remembering that you want it wet with glaze both under and on top of each piece.

10 Then continue to add the stems, the leaves, the seeds and lastly the bowl, painting on more glaze both under and over all the other pieces. When you are done, paint one final layer of glaze over the entire surface to make sure the whole of the design has been covered. Wash your brush and cup well with soap and water, and leave your decoupage panel to dry overnight.

11 Once the panel is dry, fold a piece of cardstock in half so that it matches the size of the panel and use double-sided tape to attach the panel to the front of the card.

I love the shapes that can be
found in nature – here are
a few more examples of my
decoupage designs inspired by
plants, flowers and fruit.

I am an artist living and working in the heart of the wild and beautiful Northumberland National Park.
I am grounded in this place, and much of my work and the imagery I use are linked to it. I spent ten years working as a solicitor in London, then as a complete change I embarked on an embroidery degree at Manchester Metropolitan University, where I became interested in bookbinding and papercutting.

SARAH MORPETH

Paper is my medium – everything I do begins with a blank sheet of paper. I make a range of books and works in cut paper, from unique constructed books to limited and unlimited editions and multiples and wall-hung pieces. My work combines a range of processes, including stitching, bookbinding, handpainting, printing and hand and machine cutting. I use and embrace technology, but whatever I am working on starts life as a drawing or a hand cut – or both.

My large-scale work often inspires my smaller pieces, and working with paper and book structures leads naturally to finding ways of using these to make interesting cards – with a few cuts and folds, a flat sheet of paper can become a fascinating three-dimensional space. I often use a beak book structure – as I have in this project – folded from a single piece of paper, and this becomes a little world when it is opened up.

My studio is a converted barn in rural Northumberland, where I spend a lot of time walking in the countryside, drawing and photographing as I go, and the landscape is a huge source of inspiration for my work.

TOOLS AND TECHNIQUES

The materials required for papercutting are few and relatively inexpensive. First you'll need paper. There are many different weights to choose from; I generally use 160gsm cartridge paper as it is heavy enough to stand up and to be painted – which I often do – but not so heavy that it is difficult to cut. Also essential is a scalpel – my preference is for a Swann Morton No.3 scalpel handle with easily changeable No.10A blades – and a bone folder (for nice crisp folds). It does take a little time and patience to master the papercut technique, so start with simple shapes and build up.

When designing for papercutting, it is important to make sure that some elements of the drawing overlap, so it holds together – for example, on the family of deer design, the deer are joined to each other, and key elements, such as some of the ears, are joined to the trees. This also avoids small parts of the design sticking out too far and getting damaged when the card is folded.

Once you are happy with your design, you then need to work out how the papercut will interact with the folds of the card by tracing your drawing onto folded paper and adjusting it depending on where the folds sit. Be sure to fold the card so that the pencil marks are on the inside so that they will not be visible: if you try to erase them, you risk tearing the paper.

When cutting your design, always turn the paper rather than twisting the scalpel blade. To keep your cuts clean, change your scalpel blades regularly as they do blunt quickly.

Cutting circles is the most difficult – make lots of small cuts rather than trying to cut them out in one go.

Family OF DEER
Papercut

ONE SHEET OF A3 PAPER • BONE
FOLDER • SCALPEL • METAL RULER
• CUTTING MAT • PENCIL • PUTTY
ERASER • GOUACHE OR ACRYLIC
PAINT • PAINTBRUSH

I'm inspired by the landscape and
animals around me so I decided to
base my card design on a trio of deer
that live in the woods up the hill from
my house. There's quite a knack to
designing for papercuts (see Tools and
Techniques opposite), and if you prefer
not to design your own image, you can
use the template on page 125.

1 Fold the paper in half lengthways. I use a bone
folder to get a really sharp crease.

2 Open out the sheet of paper and this time
fold it in the middle by bringing short end
to short end.

3 Open out the sheet of paper once again and turn it over. Now fold each short end to the middle fold and open back out.

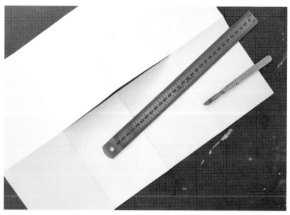

4 Using a scalpel and metal ruler, cut a straight line along the centre fold, but only along the two middle panels.

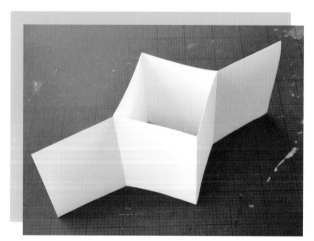

5 Refold your sheet of paper down the centre line as shown.

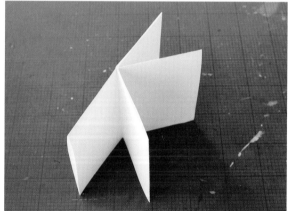

6 Now take the two wings and bring them together. The left-hand wing and the back panel then fold round to form the cover.

7 Unfold the sheet of paper so that you are working on the inside. I do this so that my pencil drawing won't be visible when the card is refolded (if you have to do a lot of rubbing out, you are likely to tear the paper). When working out your design, make sure you leave a margin at the top and bottom so that the card holds together. Design your own image or use the template on page 125.

8 Use your scalpel to carefully cut out your design, remembering to turn the paper rather than twist the scalpel to cut intricate details.

9 In this example, I have painted what will become the inside of the card (the panels behind the papercut) with gouache paint, to provide a bit of colour. If you decide to paint the background, once the paint is just dry, it's worth pressing the paper overnight under some heavy books to stop the paper wrinkling.

10 Refold the card (see steps 5 and 6). You can add a small motif to the front panel of the cover as I have here – I usually use a detail taken from my papercut design and I have cut a deer from gouache painted paper.

The beak book structure lends itself to all sorts of variations. In the Hedgerow card, pictured top, I've printed details from a pen and ink drawing of mine to form a background, and the black provides a striking contrast. In Hedgerow Hares, not only have I painted the background but I've cut a design from it too.

I began printmaking over 15 years ago, training at the Slade School of Fine Art, then completing a MA-level diploma in drawing at the Royal Drawing School. I have recently relocated from London to rural Northamptonshire, where I have my own print studio. My working week is divided between teaching printmaking at the Royal Drawing School and my studio work.

SAM MARSHALL

Linocut is a relief printmaking technique: an image is carved, using knives, chisels and gouges, into a sheet of linoleum or, as I use, a sheet of Japanese vinyl; the remaining raised areas then form the relief block to which ink is applied with a roller. A sheet of paper is pressed against the inked surface of the block using either a printing press or by hand burnishing, and only the raised part of the block deposits the ink onto the paper. If applying colour to your print, more than one lino block will need to be carved.

Once I have finished a series of linocut prints, I take an overview of the whole project and there are always a couple of designs that I feel would translate well into a card. I then redesign them, redrawing and resizing to create the new images. I then recarve these designs from Japanese vinyl to create new blocks ready to handprint the cards.

I am very fortunate as I have a purpose-built studio in my garden dedicated to printmaking. I have two printing presses – a small wooden lever press used just for linocuts and a larger traditional etching press that I use for printing both my etchings and my linocuts.

TOOLS AND TECHNIQUES

A linocut print is easy to create and doesn't require elaborate equipment – you can do it all on your kitchen table!

To create your linocut print you will first need a sheet of lino: I use a type of lino called Japanese vinyl – it's much easier to cut than traditional lino and has the advantage of being able to be carved on both sides. To carve your linocut, you will also need a selection of tools: you can buy a starter linocut tool kit from most art stores and this will include a handle and a variety of blades/gouges that will carve the block in different ways. Typically the set will include V-gouges and U-gouges and they all make different marks depending on how you use them; for example, a V-gouge will make

A selection of mushroom-handled linocut tools (V-gouges and U-gouges) and a roller or brayer.

a very fine line if you use just the tip, but if you
carve deeper it will make a thicker line.

Next in your essential kit is ink. I use Caligo
inks which are oil based but water soluble – so
you have the advantage of creating a rich, good-
quality print that's easy to clean up afterwards.
However, any block printing, water-soluble ink
can be used. You will also need a roller (often
called a brayer) to roll out your ink.

Finally you will need a tool to handprint your
linocut with. I recommend that you use either
a wooden spoon or a bamboo barren – this is a
lightweight disc covered with bamboo that allows
you to apply firm pressure across a wide area.

I get great pleasure from carving the blocks – I
find it very meditative and calming. And when
it comes to printing the image it's always full of
surprises – you can never entirely predict what
you will see when you pull back the print!

MY INSPIRATIONS

Animals form the basis of most
of my work – the more bizarre
the better! My inspiration comes
from many sources: the margins of
medieval illuminated manuscripts
and bestiaries, animal prints from
the 1800s, folk art, antique children's
books, as well as real animals
that have something of the unusual
about them. Besides Eric Ravilious,
Edward Bawden and Thomas
Bewick, I also love the work of the
19th-century ceramist William De
Morgan, particularly his fantastical
animals and birds.

There are many stages to go through until I'm
happy with a final design: I draw, redraw and
experiment with lots of different colours.

Hopping HARE

Linocut Print

TWO A5 SHEETS OF LINO OR JAPANESE VINYL • DRAWING PAPER • TRACING PAPER • PENCIL • PERMANENT MARKER • ONE A4 SHEET OF 300gsm PAPER/CARD • LARGE SHEET OF GREYBOARD OR MOUNTBOARD • METAL RULER • SCALPEL • CUTTING MAT • LINOCUT TOOLS • PROTECTIVE SURFACE • ROLLERS • PALETTE KNIFE • CALIGO INK IN BLACK AND TWO COLOURS OF YOUR CHOOSING • BAMBOO BARREN OR SPOON FOR HANDPRINTING

The Hopping Hare card requires two lino blocks to be carved – one to print the main image (the hare in black) and one to print the background colours. The colour block is inked up and printed first, then the main image is printed on top of the background colours. The hopping hare design is one of a series of linocuts I am working on at the moment featuring animals in landscapes.

1 Draw around one of your A5 lino blocks onto a sheet of drawing paper and create your design within the borders. Transfer the design onto tracing paper, then use the traced image to transfer your card design onto one of the lino blocks. You can go over the pencil drawing with a permanent marker to make the design clearer and therefore easier to cut.

2 Make a registration sheet from greyboard – this is to ensure that the lino blocks line up correctly onto your card when printing. Place your sheet of A4 card in the middle of the greyboard and draw around it, then remove. Place your lino block at the bottom of the outline and draw around it (see photo), then remove. Using a metal ruler and a scalpel, cut out the lino block shape. Check that the lino block fits snugly into the cut-out shape.

▲ Draw outline of A4 card onto greyboard.

▼ Draw outline of lino block.

3 Now begin to carve the main image block. Take care when working with linocut tools as they are sharp – always carve away from you. You will be carving away the areas you want to remain white on your print, or 'cutting away the negative'. Work slowly and carefully: you can always cut away more, but once you have cut something off you can't put it back! To carve larger areas, use a wide U-gouge, and for finer detail, use the smallest of your V-gouges. You can take proofs during the carving stage to see how your image is progressing (see steps 4 and 5 for how to do this).

4 Once you are happy with your carved block, it's time to transfer your main image to the remaining lino sheet in preparation to carve the background block. First, ink up your carved lino block. Squeeze black ink onto a protective surface – glass, Perspex, messy mat, etc. – and use a palette knife, then your roller to spread the ink into a small rectangle. Roll the roller over your carved block – it will take several passes to ensure the block is evenly inked.

5 Place your inked-up main image lino block in the precut slot in the registration sheet and place a sheet of A4 paper on top. Use a bamboo barren or the back of a spoon to gently burnish the lino block, thus transferring the image to the paper.

6 Peel back the paper to reveal your print.

7 Now remove the main image lino block and replace it with the remaining lino sheet. Relay your print onto the registration sheet so that the printed image is laid over the lino sheet. Gently burnish to transfer the image from the paper onto the lino.

8 Remove the lino from the registration sheet and use a permanent maker to draw out the areas where you want your colours to be.

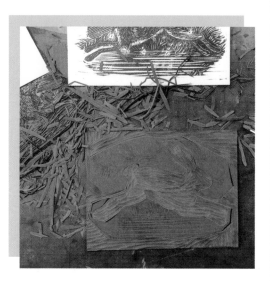

9 Now create the colour background block by carving away the lino to leave just those marked out areas in relief to apply your colour inks onto.

10 Prepare your inks – I have chosen green ink for the top area of the background and blue ink for the lower area. Using a different roller for each colour, roll the inks onto the background block .

11 You are now ready to begin printing your card(s). Place your inked-up background block into the slot in the registration sheet, place a sheet of A4 card on top and burnish the block. Carefully lift to reveal your printed background.

12 Repeat steps 10 and 11 as many times as you require, depending on how many cards you want to make. Allow the prints to dry for a day or so, hanging them up if possible, before going on to print the main image block on top of the colour background.

13 To complete the printing of the card, ink-up the main image block with black ink and place it in the registration sheet. Place the background-printed card onto the registration sheet so that the printed area lies over the lino block; burnish the back of the card then carefully peel it back to reveal your final print.

14 Repeat step 13 on each print. Leave the finished prints to dry for at least 24 hours, then fold each in half to produce the finished card.

Many of my card designs are made from just one linocut block and a small selection of these is shown below. All of these cards feature animals that are characters in my larger, more detailed prints, for example, Fennec Fox, top, features in my Siberian Jerboa linocut.

I am a mixed-media artist living in Cornwall who is lucky enough to earn a living by creating work from driftwood and other stuff that's free! Although I studied illustration and printmaking at art school, I knew it wasn't a career I wanted to pursue: I love the freedom you get from working with found objects; I love that there are no boundaries in my line of work.

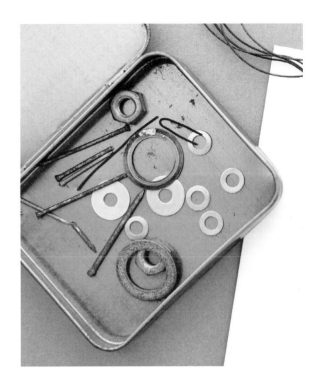

KIRSTY ELSON

In common with other mixed-media artists, I see treasure where others may see only trash. Found objects, be they gathered from a walk on the beach or a rummage at the bottom of a tool box, can be transformed into something amazing. Materials that many people wouldn't look at twice speak to me and I am totally guided by the everyday objects I find and I am rarely stuck for inspiration. People often send me things in the post; these acts of kindness can result in my best work as often they are not the kind of things I would happen upon and they get me thinking out of the box. As an artist, you want to be constantly evolving and using unique found materials is my way of doing this.

I started out making handmade cards when I began my business well over a decade ago now. From there, it seemed like a natural progression to then make more three-dimensional pieces. I don't make handmade cards to sell these days – the cards I produce now are printed ones from original works, such as my ambulance card pictured at the end of this chapter.

in my studio

I have two workrooms – all my tools (saws, drills, sanders) are in the shed, so the heavy-duty work happens there. It's very dusty! Then I have a small room indoors where I paint and add the finishing touches – my favourite bit!

MY INSPIRATIONS

I grew up by the sea in Devon and I am very much influenced by my local surroundings here in Cornwall: the sights, the smells, the sounds of the sea are a constant source of inspiration to me and the waves wash up an ever-changing stock of materials on a daily basis. No two pieces of driftwood are ever the same. It has a lovely worn quality and layers of peeling paint that you simply cannot emulate; add the element of unknown history and it becomes even more exciting.

I adore the work of Edwina Bridgeman who makes delightful art using a whole array of 'rubbish' she picks up, including wood, metal, paper and textiles. I've been fortunate enough to take part in a couple of her workshops and she is brilliant – a real inspiration!

I have an ever-expanding collection of rusty nails, screws and washers, so I thought I'd use some of these to design my Recycled Bike card.

TOOLS AND TECHNIQUES

Essential tools for working with found objects such as those used for the Recycled Bike card can be found in the average tool box: pliers, wire cutters, tin snips, small hammer. When creating your own version of the design, you are likely to need several pairs of scissors (for paper/fabric, etc.) and a good adhesive. I find the best glue to use for a project like this is a small tube of superglue with a little nozzle to prevent too much glue seeping everywhere.

Recycled BIKE

Found Objects Art

PENCIL • PAPER • PRE-FOLDED BASE CARD MEASURING 13.5cm SQUARE, MINIMUM 240gsm • SELECTION OF OLD METAL TACKS, NAILS, WASHERS, WIRE, ETC. (FOR MY DESIGN I USED THREE WASHERS, THREE NAILS AND A SMALL PIECE OF RUSTY WIRE) • WIRE CUTTERS • PLIERS • SLIVER OF WOOD • CAMERA • ERASER • GOOD-QUALITY SUPERGLUE • FABRIC REMNANT (OR COLOURED PAPER)

My Recycled Bike card was made using little odds and ends I found in my tool box. I had the idea for using washers for wheels and it grew from there. I like to include bikes in my work – very simplified ones – so it seemed like an obvious choice. Be inspired by what you find in your tool box to make your very own model, and feel free to add your own components or substitute materials – this is a merely a guide. I want you to have fun!

1 First decide on your design. I've made a fairly traditional bicycle, but you could choose a mountain or racing bike, retro-style chopper or even a penny-farthing. Keep the outline design pretty simple and don't be tempted to get carried away with too many tiny details.

2 Once you're happy with your design, draw it very lightly in pencil on the front of your card, trying to make it as central as possible.

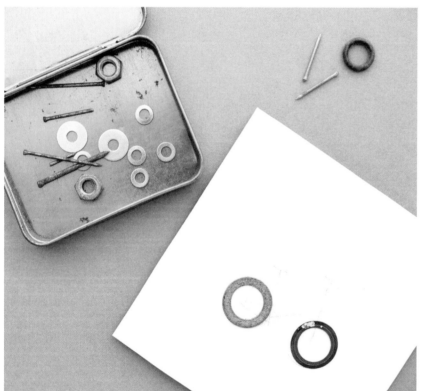

3 Now build your bike from your tool box bits and pieces – at this stage you are just compiling, not gluing. Starting with the wheels, use your pencil drawing as a guide to find what size washers work for your bicycle design (I found thin washers were best). Then decide on the nails you'll need to make the three main parts of the frame, again using your drawing as your guide. If the nails are too long, you can trim them down with wire cutters.

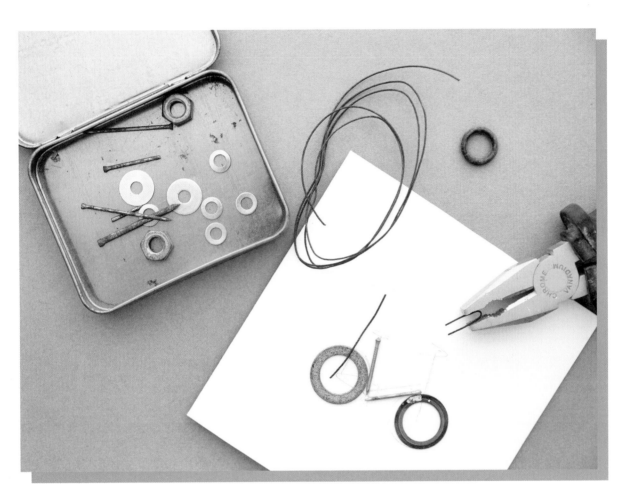

4 Use wire cutters to cut a small piece of wire for the handlebars and bend into shape using pliers. Make the bike chain in the same way, this time using a slightly longer length of wire. Use a small washer for the chain ring and place it where the chain meets the frame. Your bicycle is beginning to take shape and the next thing is to find a tiny sliver of wood for the saddle.

5 Once all your bike components have been assembled, take a reference photo before sticking each piece in place. Working on one piece at a time, remove the bike part and rub out that area of the pencil drawing (this can be fiddly). Carefully apply superglue to the bike part and secure it onto your card. It is a good idea to wait for each piece to dry before applying the next as it can get messy otherwise. Repeat until each component is stuck down. Now add the finishing details – I've made a jolly flag from wire and a tiny fabric remnant. Alternatively, you could add a basket to the handlebars. Feel free to make it your own!

Two examples of my printed cards. The left-hand one shows a typical 3D scene made from driftwood and other found materials. The right-hand one is my popular 'Get Well Soon' card. I had been experimenting making little trucks using vintage tins, washers and painted driftwood, and when I found this old plaster tin, I had the idea of making it into an ambulance.

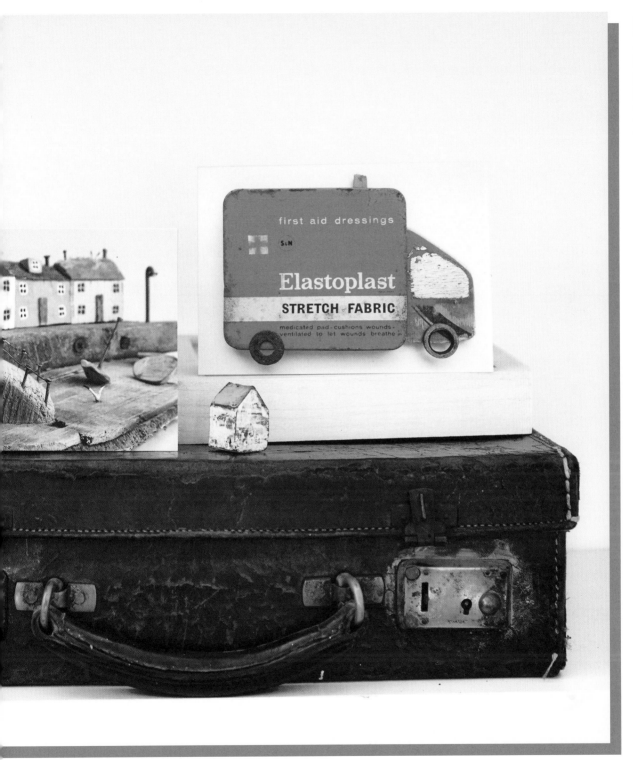

Originally from Buenos Aires, Argentina, I have lived in south London since graduating from Camberwell College of Arts in the nineties. I come from a background in ceramics and printmaking, and my work has always featured layered images together with bright colour and surface decoration. In recent years, my work has focused on collage and decoupage using old photographs, drawings and other found imagery, and I produce a range of items with these media including cards, prints, scarves, upcycled furniture and decorative objects.

GABRIELA SZULMAN

My work draws on nostalgia and the reassembly of found images, so collage is an ideal medium to use. The term collage originates from the French verb *coller*, meaning 'to glue', and images are cut out and glued together to create new and often surprising designs. I love delving into old photograph albums, vintage documents, magazines and books, knitting patterns and scraps of writing. These provide me with a wealth of imagery that I can just as easily use on a small card, a pair of shoes or a piece of furniture.

I find that creating cards is a great way of trying out and developing ideas, and of discovering how a new collection may work: often something that starts life as a greeting card will later morph into a large print or even a scarf. Cards are also the cheapest items I make so they make great 'impulse buys'!

My home is a 'live-work' unit in Camberwell, south London, where I am very lucky to have a large double-height studio and office, a space in which I make, teach small groups and have a permanent display of my work.

TOOLS AND TECHNIQUES

The wonderful thing about the technique of collage is that no specialist equipment is required. Magazines, picture books and photographs are great sources of imagery and inspiration, and no doubt you will have at least some of these at home, or could collect them easily. Other essentials include small-bladed scissors and a scalpel knife for intricate cutting out, and a cutting mat, of course. You'll also need glue – I use Mod Podge but any water-based glue should work – and a brush to apply it with. Optional pieces of equipment are a scanner and a printer, but the scanner can be easily replaced by a good-quality camera and the printer by a photocopier.

I get most of my old books and cards from markets stalls and charity shops. Ask friends and family to keep interesting stuff for you – some of my best resources are things that were given to me.

MY INSPIRATIONS

My grandmother's women's magazines, handwritten letters, Victoriana, technical manuals and illustrated dictionaries, among many other things; second-hand bookshops, junk shops, market stalls, attics and long-forgotten boxes are my treasure trove: I often find inspiration in those things that other people discard. I live in a quirky and diverse part of London, where just a walk to the shops of Peckham or Brixton can fire the spark that starts my next creative project. Looking to the art world, I admire and am inspired by the work of American artist Joseph Cornell, one of the pioneers of assemblage in the 20th century.

My sketchbooks are where I play and develop ideas that may later find their way into my work.

WINGED Lady

Collage

BOOKS, MAGAZINES AND PATTERNED PAPERS • SCANNER, PRINTER AND INKJET PAPER (OPTIONAL) • SCISSORS • CUTTING MAT • SCALPEL • METAL RULER • PENCIL • ONE A4 SHEET OF 300gsm CARD • FLAT PAINTBRUSH • WATER-BASED GLUE

My card project is a collage of a winged lady wearing a colourful dress that I have made using some favourite found images, patterned paper and book pages. I have been making art dolls and little brooches with fairy images for a while now; this collage was inspired by those and now forms part of the same collection.

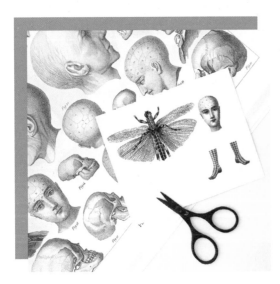

1 Gather a selection of magazines, books and patterned papers to look for images. As you are making a winged lady, you need to find three components: face, wings and legs. Also you'll need patterned paper for the crown and dress, and stamps or small details to embellish the dress.

2 If the images you want to use come from books or other publications you want to keep pristine, scan and edit using Photoshop or other software and then print to size on inkjet paper before cutting out. Bear in mind that if you have scanned images you'll be able to use them again to make a series of cards.

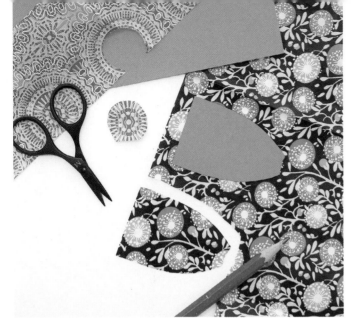

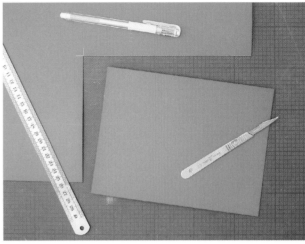

3 Draw a simple shape for the dress and a circle slightly larger than the head for the crown onto a piece of card, cut them out and use as templates to mark and cut out the patterned paper. (Keep these card templates if you plan to make more cards with the same motif.) Cut a 10cm x 2cm strip of lettering from a book or magazine.

4 To make the base card, cut a piece of card measuring 21cm x 15cm from your sheet of 300gsm card. Fold the card in half widthways to create a card measuring 10.5cm x 15cm, which fits into a standard C5 envelope, and open it out again.

5 Arrange all the shapes on the front (right-hand) panel of your base card, ensuring that the whole figure is centred. Make pencil marks on top of the crown, under the strip and at the widest point of the wings: this will ensure that you can glue the shapes exactly where they need to go after you've removed them.

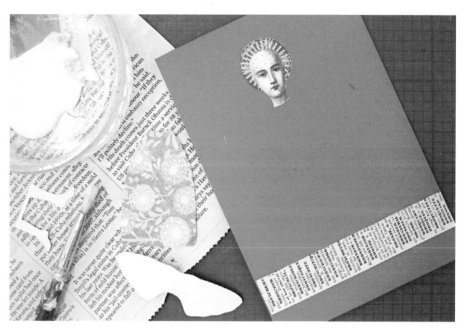

6 Turn all the shapes upside down and paint each one in turn with a very thin layer of glue, using a flat brush. It is important to keep the layer of glue very thin and to cover the whole surface. Glue the shapes in order: strip, crown, head, feet, wings and dress. Press each shape from the centre out to the sides to make sure there are no air bubbles.

7 Add a detail to the dress, for example, a small flower, a circle or a stamp. Once the card is completely dry, refold and place it under a pile of books for an hour or so to flatten. Choose a standard C5 envelope in a contrasting colour and your card is ready to be sent.

As so often happens in my work, other things I already make inspired this project. Last year I created a collection of decorative dolls to hang on the wall and brooches shaped like miniature fairies; I had been thinking of complementing these with greeting cards or prints and the winged lady collage card was the first step in that direction. I tried different combinations of components until I found one that worked well as a collage. Once the basic composition was established, I developed a series of cards using the same image on different colour backgrounds, using different papers for the dress to make each unique.

I recently graduated from Nottingham Trent University and although my background is in graphic design, I found my passion for illustration in my final year there. My work often features a range of techniques and I like to experiment with different types of mark making, including ink and pen, painting, papercutting and stitch. What these processes have in common are that they focus on attention to detail and are very often hand-crafted.

LUCY FEATHERSTONE

I have always been interested in pushing my creative boundaries. When I was exploring creating machine-stitched illustrations, I found that although I was able to achieve some lovely results I wanted to produce pictures with a bit more control and accuracy, so I developed my technique of handstitch art. It is more time-consuming and requires more patience – along with copious amounts of tea – but the result is something far more beautiful. It creates such delicate crisp lines, and the use of popping colour thread vividly brings illustrations to life.

In the final year of my studies, I was presented with a project to create a greeting card that challenges the current perception of cards. In my research I found that a handmade gift was appreciated far more than something that had been commercially manufactured. I discovered that people are more likely to display and keep a greeting card that has been beautifully crafted, and this was the starting point for my handstitch art technique.

I don't actually have my own studio at the moment as I work full time (I'm a junior designer for Campbell Books where my creativity is challenged on an everyday basis to devise engaging novelty books for toddlers!). But what I love about stitching is that you can take it with you wherever you go, and I am often seen sewing my illustrations on my commute to work.

TOOLS AND TECHNIQUES

When I am developing an idea for a card design, I always start by making a few detailed sketches, often researching some visual references to inspire me. I begin with an outline of the object, and then I plan out where I want my thread lines to appear within the image and I start to sketch these in also. This then helps me work out where the stitching holes need to be placed, which I begin to pencil in. (This is a very important stage as when I start threading, it is very hard to redo once a hole has been pierced in the paper.)

I usually use a relatively thick piece of paper for my cards. I love the quality and finish of the 'Accent Fresco' range by G.F. Smith, choosing only white or cream coloured paper so that the coloured threads stand out well. When selecting paper remember it must be strong enough to be able to have stitching holes pierced into it without tearing, but not so thick that you find it tricky to punch a needle through – so nothing heavier than 300gsm.

For the stitching I use polyester clothing thread or all-purpose thread. I like to use at least one metallic thread in my illustrations as it adds a nice finish to the picture. Gutermann threads have a lovely selection of metallics, as well as brightly coloured threads. I usually buy an assorted selection of steel hand-sewing needles and use the smallest in width, nothing larger than 0.2mm. This ensures that the stitching holes are quite discrete (you don't want the holes in the paper to be too large as the paper is liable to tear if the holes are too close together).

RIGHT These pages from my sketchbooks show how I developed my designs. I love the challenge of creating new illustrations. As the threads are laid down in straight lines it can be quite testing to produce curves and circles, but it is worth the effort as there is nothing quite like a handstitched art card.

MY INSPIRATIONS

I really appreciate the little things when it comes to design and I am influenced by the detail in everything. Wherever I go I pick up anything I find inspirational, whether it be a quirky leaflet or a beautifully illustrated postcard, and I keep it all in a scrapbook so I can refer back to it whenever I want – it's like my own 'hands-on' Pinterest, which I am also an avid fan of!

I am always amazed by the work of Yulia Brodskaya, a quilling artist whose handcrafted talent truly inspires me, and her technique of using paper to draw with would amaze anyone.

Polyester clothing thread or all-purpose thread guides through the paper better than cotton thread and it doesn't break as easily.

OUT OF *this* world
Handstitch Art

PENCIL • PAPER • TRACING PAPER • PRE-FOLDED BASE CARD MEASURING 15cm SQUARE, MINIMUM 300gsm• BLACK MARKER PEN • SCISSORS • SEWING NEEDLE • THREADS IN COLOURS OF YOUR CHOOSING (I HAVE USED LIGHT GREY, RED AND ORANGE, AND SILVER METALLIC) • CLEAR ADHESIVE TAPE

The Out of This World rocket card is a great design to get started on the path to creating your own handstitch art. The beauty of this project is that although it may look quite complicated, it is actually an easy pattern to get used to the pierce/stitch technique as only straight triangular shapes are used to make up the design. If this is your first attempt at handstitch art, you may want to use the template provided on page 124 although the process of creating the design from scratch is described in the steps below.

1 Start by sketching the outline of your planned design onto a spare piece of paper; sketch in where the lines of thread will go, along with any areas of block (unstitched) colour you want to add. (In this design, I have used block colour for the two exhausts.) Now start putting dots where each of the thread lines end, making these a bit darker so they stand out when it comes to tracing your design. Take your tracing paper and trace all of the dots (needle holes) of your design. Transfer your tracing onto the back of the front panel of your base card. Before you begin stitching, punch through each of the holes with your needle as shown – this makes the sewing process easier.

2 Refold your base card. Use the black marker pen to colour in the two exhausts at the base of the rocket on the front of the card, and then you are ready to begin stitching.

3 I usually start stitching at the top of the design, in this case the tip of the rocket (light grey thread). I usually work with a metre length of thread in my needle but choose a length that you prefer (you can always rethread). A good starting hole is one you might be continuously threading through within your design, for example the tip of the rocket nose. Pull the threaded needle through from the back to the front of the card and secure the end of the thread with tape on the inside of the front panel.

4 Pull the attached thread across the front of the card and pass the needle through your second hole, ensuring the thread is pulled tight. In this case we are going to start by threading the line of holes just below the tip of the rocket, therefore the second hole would be the hole at the far right of the row. Pull your thread back through the starting hole at the tip of the rocket nose triangle. (Note: for each triangular shape that makes up the rocket design, you will continue to pass your thread through the starting hole for that section of the design.) Repeat this sequence until all the holes are threaded in the first section of your design, finishing on the inside panel. Cut the thread and attach the end with tape as in step 3.

5 Now move on to stitch the left-hand and right-hand sides of the rocket body (also light grey thread). Before you start stitching, count along the holes pierced at the base of the rocket and slightly mark the middle hole (this will be the starting hole for the metallic thread triangle – middle panel – of the rocket body, which will be stitched in step 6). Working on the left-hand side first, start stitching from your starting hole (far left hole on the base row of the rocket nose) to the far left hole on the left-hand side, continuing to thread all the holes from the outside in, leaving the marked (middle) hole unstitched. Repeat to stitch the right-hand side of the rocket body, again remembering to leave the middle hole unstitched.

6 Stitch the middle panel of the rocket body with silver metallic thread. Your starting hole is the marked (middle) hole left unsewn when working the side panels of the rocket body; thread through all the holes in the row above to join them to the top triangle (rocket nose). Working with metallic thread can be rather difficult as it tends to fray a lot more easily than regular thread, so I only use this thread in small proportions when planning out my design. Pull metallic thread through the holes gently.

7 The rocket body is now complete, so move on to stitch the rocket wings with red thread. Two triangle sections are stitched to make each rocket wing.

8 Now work the fire coming from each exhaust using orange thread. Your starting hole will be the single pierced hole at the base of the exhaust: you will be stitching a stretched diamond shape; begin stitching the left-hand side first, then work your way back up on the right-hand side.

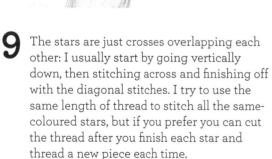

9 The stars are just crosses overlapping each other: I usually start by going vertically down, then stitching across and finishing off with the diagonal stitches. I try to use the same length of thread to stitch all the same-coloured stars, but if you prefer you can cut the thread after you finish each star and thread a new piece each time.

10 The inside front panel of your card is now really quite messy with all those taped down thread ends. To finish the card, you can cut a piece of paper 15cm square and stick it to the inside front panel to hide your 'workings'.

When stitching a circle, you can make your rows of holes close or far apart depending on your preferred width for the aperture. From any hole, stitch diagonally across the circle, coming back up through the hole next to the starting hole in a clockwise direction; then go back through the hole next to your second hole and contine clockwise around the entire circle. Repeat to stitch all the holes around the circle in an anticlockwise direction. Experiment to create other curved shapes including teardrops and semicircles.

I am a surface pattern designer with a
degree in printed textiles and surface pattern
design from Leeds College of Art. I have
my own company, Jessica Hogarth Designs,
and I split my time between illustrating for
commercial clients and designing and selling
my own range of paper and textile products,
which includes an extensive greeting card
collection. I love both architecture and
the coast and these are themes that often
feature in my designs. As I live and work by
the sea, I am never far away from views that
inspire me.

JESSICA HOGARTH

My work is illustrative and focused around linear designs that are
always hand-drawn to begin with before being digitally enhanced with
colour. I love working in this way: it allows me to be creative as I hand-
draw all of my designs, but ultimately I can produce a finished design
that has the potential to be printed in many different ways. It is possible
to manipulate a digital file in order to make templates for other print
processes besides digital print, such as silkscreen printing for example,
which can give more options if taking a product to mass manufacture.

The wholesale side of my business is focused around selling multiple
pieces of the same design to retailers, so this method of working
ensures that once the time has been committted to designing the
artwork, the process of turning the art into a digitally printed finished
card is significantly less than with other processes that involve more
manual labour, such as hand-colouring.

in my studio

After two years working from a home studio, I finally moved into a larger space in the seaside town of Whitby in North Yorkshire. My new studio is a place designed to enable me to hold more stock as well as providing me with the perfect workspace to create new patterns and designs.

TOOLS AND TECHNIQUES

In the world of commercial design today, digital illustration is very important; possessing this skill has allowed me to work with a wide variety of companies both in the UK and further afield as I can simply email them a print-ready artwork file. My card project is a great introduction to show you how you can turn a hand-drawn illustration into a digital design. The beauty with artwork of this nature is that there are no constraints as to the number of colours used and the finished design can easily be altered in size.

You can edit an image in a number of computer programs. Many artists use Adobe Photoshop, but I prefer Adobe Illustrator. Illustrator lends itself perfectly to creating digital artwork as it is vector based. This means that you can create completely smooth lines and graphics without any pixelation (loss of image quality) no matter what size your design. Photoshop, on the other hand, is pixel based, so artwork will begin to lose its quality if you keep making it larger. While Photoshop is excellent for combining some graphic work with photography, for example, or tidying up a watercolour image for reproduction, I find Illustrator is easier to use when working with a line drawing and colouring it with a block colour, as I have done with my Beach Huts card. The effects you can achieve in either program will depend on your familiarity with it and your skill level. It is worth exploring the program options before you invest – 30-day free trials are available at Adobe (adobe.com). You will also find an abundance of tutorials on YouTube.

MY INSPIRATIONS

Pinterest is my go-to place to look at beautiful imagery when I am working from my desk. I find it really inspirational to soak up other illustration work, colour palettes and photos when considering my direction for a new project. However, it is important not to be influenced too closely by existing artwork, and you should always strive for your idea to be unique. Many artists will have used the seaside as inspiration, but try to find your own style to express your ideas.

One of the most inspirational artists for me is Anna Bond of Florida-based Rifle Paper Co. She retails a broad range of products including many greeting cards. Her approach to design is very different to mine as she does a lot of painting with gouache. But the overall look and branding of her company, particularly her use of colour, is incredibly sophisticated and unique.

I love my seaside studio but whenever I can I like to get away and have first-hand experiences of new places.

My light, bright seaside studio, where I create all my design work.

Beach HUTS

Digital Illustration

TWO SHEETS OF A4 COPY PAPER • PENCIL • ERASER • RULER • TRACING PAPER • BLACK FINE LINER PEN • MASKING TAPE • LIGHT BOX • COMPUTER AND SCANNER • ADOBE ILLUSTRATOR SOFTWARE • PRINTER • ONE SHEET OF CARD FOR PRINTING YOUR DESIGN ONTO (THICK ENOUGH FOR THE FOLDED CARD TO STAND UP BUT THIN ENOUGH TO GO THROUGH YOUR PRINTER) • SCISSORS, OR CRAFT KNIFE • CUTTING MAT

This project has been inspired by my love of the seaside and the surroundings in which I live. Utilising photos found online, I have been able to come up with an artwork layout that is unique and personal to me. The majority of my work is developed using the process we are working with here, which is digitally enhancing a hand-drawn line illustration with flat block colours. I like to use a mixture of block colour shapes, such as the clouds, then line drawings that are filled with colour, such as the beach huts themselves. My card has been created using a combination of hand-drawing and digital manipulation using Adobe Illustrator.

1 Gather your inspiration, whether it be physical or digital: think about colour palettes, a scene or specific theme you would like to illustrate and how you want the finished card to look.

2 Take a sheet of A4 copy paper and use a pencil to draw a 12cm x 17cm portrait rectangle onto it (a common standard size for greeting cards). Sketch your proposed illustration within the marked out space, extending your sketch lines by a few millimetres beyond the box lines; this will ensure that when you come to print your design, you can crop it to fill the whole space. Your pencil drawing doesn't have to be perfect, just good enough for you to trace your refined version over the top of it – see step 3.

3 Once you are happy with your sketched design, the next stage is to trace over your pencil drawing using a pen. Place your sketched illustration onto your light box, or tape it to a brightly lit window, and lay a second sheet of A4 copy paper over the top of it, lining them up at the edges. Use masking tape to hold the paper in place so that the top sheet doesn't move around as you draw. Using a black fine liner pen this time, draw a final refined version of your sketch using the pencil outlines beneath to guide you.

4 Your design is now ready to transfer to the computer using a scanner. A black outline is easier to work from than a pencil drawing as the lines are clearer, darker and easier to manipulate in the computer program. (Note: if you find you have made a mistake on your drawing, you could use the rubber and pen tool in Photoshop to tidy your artwork up before opening it in Illustrator.)

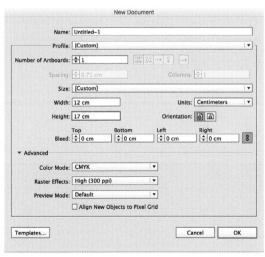

5 Open up Illustrator and go to File ▶ New. A box will come up with various options for your document settings. For colour mode, select CMYK, which is important for printing your end result onto paper or card. Select a document size and orientation. Ensure that the orientation is set to portrait and that the document unit is cm (centimetres). For width enter 12 and for height enter 17 and then click OK at the bottom right of the box.

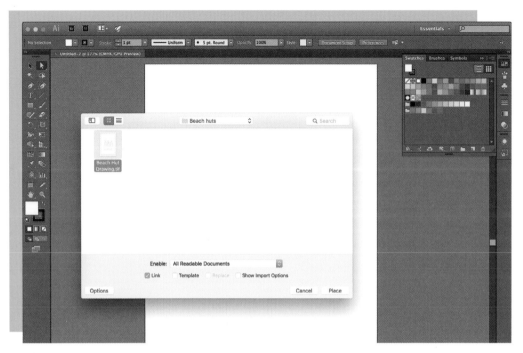

6 Go to File ▶ Place and then select your image from its location on your computer and click Place at the bottom right of the box.

7 With your image selected, go to Image Trace. Note: the default trace usually works just fine for a line drawing, but if you don't get the results you want, you can explore the image trace options. (I tend to use an image tolerance of around 175, but it very much depends on the thickness of your drawn line and the complexity of the illustration.)

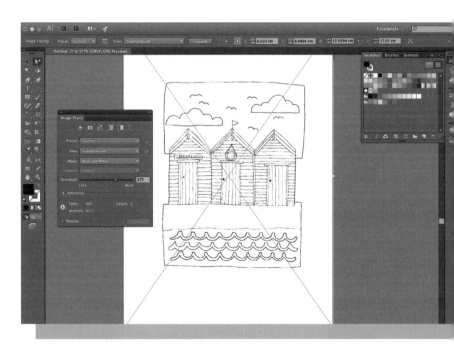

8 Now select Object ▶ Expand from the menu at the top to make your document into a vector graphic. (If you click on the image it will now show the results of the conversion to vector graphic.) There will be a white box around your image. If you right click on the image (with it still selected) you can select 'ungroup'. The white box around your image is the rest of the A4 paper that was not drawn on. Simply click on this white space and hit the backspace button to delete it. Now go to Select ▶ All at the top of the document and then click on your illustration and move it to where you would like it to be positioned on the document: only the image within this rectangle will print and ideally it should be centralised so it prints as a complete rectangle with perfect edges.

9 Now that you have turned your image into a vector graphic, it is time to colourise it. Select sections of the illustration and add colour by either utilising the existing palette or making your own. If you go to Window ▶ Swatches, a box full of colour chips pops up. You can use the colours already available or make your own: press the new swatch button and play around with the colour bars to create your desired shade. Pictured left is the image part way through the colourising process.

10 Once the colourised image is complete, be sure to save your work. You can then return to it at a later date to print more cards, changing the colours if you choose to, or altering the size of the image for other purposes. The beauty of artwork that is in 'vector' format is that you can make it whatever size you want and it will never pixelate, meaning that the image will always look sharp.

11 Print your design onto your A4 card in the format shown, allowing for the card to be folded in half.

12 Trim the card to 24cm x 17cm and fold it in the centre to make a card 12cm x 17cm; this will fit a 12.5cm x 17.5cm envelope perfectly.

Here are two more typical examples of my style of work, featuring linear illustrations filled with colour. Unlike the Beach Hut card, these two cards were drawn at a larger scale and made smaller for the final design. The main benefit of working in this way is that the illustrations can be made more detailed. I will often opt to draw elements separately and place them in the final layout once I am working in Illustrator, as manipulation of a design layout is much easier if the elements are drawn separately. This gives me the option to change the layout on screen from my original concept should I choose to. As you become familiar with the Adobe Illustrator program, these are options you can explore for yourself.

I grew up in Australia where I studied printmaking at the University of Southern Queensland. I now live and work in London, and from working on paper, I've transitioned to printing on fabric. I enjoy the textural element as well as the creative potential for the printed fabric, and through my company, Black Cactus London, I create unique handprinted art and accessories inspired by nature.

ANNA JACKSON

Textile foiling is a screen-print technique but instead of screen printing ink onto your fabric background, you screen print the adhesive for the foil to stick to. Once the adhesive is dry, the foil is applied with a hot iron and the top layer is peeled away to reveal a lush metallic surface. I love the spontaneity of handprinting and I am a fan of 'happy accidents' although my aim is always to create texture upon the printed surface. Textile foiling enhances the surface of fabric with cracks, marks and beautifully reflective angles.

Nature is my greatest inspiration and leaves are currently the strongest theme in my work. Each leaf is one of a kind and serves as a reminder of how remarkable even the small things around us are, a feeling I hope the recipient shares when they receive a textile-foiled handprinted card. Making cards helps me to try out new designs and ideas on a small scale; it gives me the freedom to work on a piece just for the enjoyment of the creative process without worrying about how it ties into a larger body of work. When making cards you are free to experiment, make mistakes and learn new techniques without too much investment in time or materials.

All my pieces are created in my south London studio, and although I live and work in such a built-up place, it's important for me to retain a strong connection with nature. My personal focus remains on seeking out the green spaces and nature's presence within our urban streets, through the trees and the plants and even the weeds that grow here.

Metallic foils are available online in a wide range of colours and textures. Start with a sample pack to try the effects of different foil types before investing in quantity.

TOOLS AND TECHNIQUES

The idea for using leaves as templates came to me when I first moved into my own print studio. I wanted interesting ways to print without the need for expensive equipment and lots of space, both of which are required to produce traditional photo-stencil screens and designs. Overprinting the surrounding area with foiling is a beautiful way to frame the image and prevents the fabric from fraying when cut, so it's practical too. I never tire of peeling away the foil to see the results.

This technique can be done on your kitchen table using found objects with minimal clean up. You'll need an A4 silkscreen and a squeegee, both affordable items that can be reused for any other screen-print projects. You can buy a ready-made stretched silkscreen on a frame in different sizes, and these will last you a long time if cleaned after each printing session. When printing on fabric you need a silkscreen with a low mesh count to allow more of the ink, or adhesive in this case, to pass through the screen and onto the material: I use a 55 mesh count silkscreen frame.

For your printing fabric, select a smooth fabric with a manmade fibre, a thick polyester rather than cotton, as the fabric will need to withstand being heated with a hot iron without scorching or discolouring. Always test a small piece of your chosen fabric before printing.

There are foils designed for paper and foils designed for fabric. Fabric foils are thicker, stronger and will last longer; however, for card-making, paper foil will work well and there are generally more colours available for these.

WREATH OF Leaves

Textile Foil Print

FABRIC OF YOUR CHOICE • BASE CARD 15.5cm SQUARE, APPROX 290gsm OR THICKER • NEWSPAPER • A4 SILKSCREEN FOR TEXTILES • FOUND LEAVES • FOIL ADHESIVE • SPOON • SQUEEGEE • HAIR DRYER • ROTARY CUTTER (OR A PAIR OF SHARP SCISSORS) • CUTTING MAT • RULER • METALLIC FOIL • TEA TOWEL • IRON • SPRAY MOUNT OR PAPER GLUE • BRUSH

Using real leaves you've found yourself, capture the beauty of their natural form in this richly textured wreath design. Balance the simplicity of the motif by surrounding it with a luxurious metallic surface, and remember, this card design will be unique each time you print a version of it.

1 Cut your fabric roughly 2.5cm wider on all sides than the size of your base card. Iron the fabric to ensure it is completely crease free. Place the fabric on top of some newspaper to keep your work surface clean.

2 Select your leaves and arrange them on your fabric in an attractive circular shape. Thin, flat-laying leaves will give the best result for a sharp outline. Your leaves are the stencils for your print and you will be printing the space around them in the metallic foil.

3 Carefully place your silkscreen on top of the fabric and leaves.

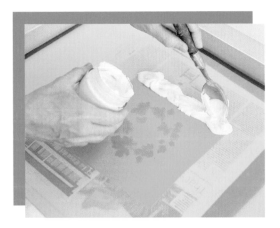

4 Use a spoon to spread foil adhesive onto the silkscreen in a line above and just wider than the fabric beneath to ensure that all the fabric is printed.

5 Hold your squeegee with both hands at a roughly 45-degree angle and firmly push and drag the squeegee across the silkscreen, working quickly and with even pressure to pass the adhesive through the screen onto your fabric.

6 Add another line of adhesive again above the fabric as in step 4 and quickly pass your squeegee over your silkscreen once more. This will ensure that you have a good, even coverage of adhesive, but don't let it get too thick.

7 Now carefully peel the fabric off the silkscreen. Before moving on to step 8, clean the silkscreen. Scrape the excess adhesive back into the pot, and wash your screen immediately with fresh water and a sponge (the adhesive is water-based so there's no need for detergent).

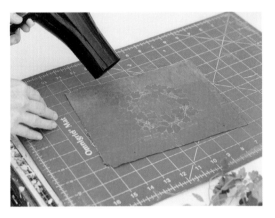

8 Allow the fabric to dry fully using a hair dryer for best results; it should be opaque and completely dry to the touch.

9 Cut your foil to the required size for the area you are printing (a rotary cutter and ruler will give crisp lines and provide the best finish for your card, but sharp scissors are fine otherwise). Place the foil coloured-side up onto the dried adhesive.

10 Set the iron to its highest temperature. Cover the fabric with a tea towel and move your iron slowly over the surface, gently and constantly, for approximately 30 seconds.

11 Allow the foiled fabric to cool for approximately a minute before carefully peeling the foil away to check on progress; if it is not lifting easily, replace the tea towel and re-iron the area. If the remaining foil looks too shiny for your taste, replace the tea towel and quickly iron it again to dull it a little.

12 Using either spray mount or paper glue, coat the back of the untrimmed printed fabric and place it onto the front panel of your base card and carefully smooth it out.

13 Turn the card over and, working on a cutting mat, trim away the overlapping edges of the foiled fabric using a rotary cutter and ruler (or use a pair of sharp scissors to trim by hand).

OPPOSITE Experiment with different-shaped leaves and colours to create your own designs. A fern frond makes a delicate and striking design especially when you print it onto a contrasting black fabric with silver foil. Geranium leaves create an attractive outline and look great in a group. Enjoy the unexpected texture and marks your prints will create. I recommend choosing darker-coloured fabrics to complement your metallic prints.

I was trained as a printmaker and I have a Bachelor of Fine Arts in printmaking from Montana State University and a Master of Fine Arts in printmaking from Louisiana State University. I continue to make fine art when I'm not busy designing and printing, as well as performing other operational tasks for my company, Blackbird Letterpress.

KATHRYN HUNTER

I enjoy the process of drawing by hand, pencil to paper, and then transforming my artwork with modern technology into a printing form. Then, I turn full circle to print my drawing on a vintage letterpress. Letterpress printing is a relief print technique, where the printing area is raised above the non-printing area: a thin layer of ink is rolled over an image/form, and then the letterpress brings the paper in contact with the image/form. Unlike other flat-printing methods, such as screen printing, for example, letterpress printing creates a physical impression in the paper, which is quite beautiful.

At Blackbird Letterpress, we specialise in designing and printing greeting cards, handmade notebooks, animal-shaped die-cut cards and paper novelties. I enjoy paper that transforms from a two-dimensional, flat form to a three-dimensional model, so many of the card prints we sell can be assembled and have parts that move. Creating a design for a DIY paper model can be complicated. It often takes a few rounds to get all the measurements correct.

I started Blackbird Letterpress in 2003 after spontaneously purchasing a Chandler and Price letterpress (circa 1904). From wedding invitations to quirky animal cards, we design and print everything in-house and our studio has three vintage presses. We are located in Baton Rouge, Louisiana, by the Mississippi River.

I printed the Camper Adventure card on a cylinder letterpress, a Vandercook SP15, using photopolymer plates.

TOOLS AND TECHNIQUES

A letterpress is a large, heavy, often expensive, piece of equipment, so if you are just getting started with this technique, you'll need to find access to a letterpress by checking into shared letterpress printshops in your area (see Suppliers).

There are different types of letterpress. A cylinder press, such as the Vandercook letterpress used to print the Camper Adventure card, 'grips' the paper and rolls it along the cylinder and over the relief image/form that is 'locked' up in the press bed. This type of press is great when printing large surface areas and flat areas of colour. Another common press is a platen press where the relief image/form and the paper are both on flat surfaces. The press moves these flat surfaces together to print. The platen press is ideal when printing in larger quantities.

Whatever the letterpress type, the relief image/form used must be *exactly* 23.3172mm in height. Traditionally, to print text, either metal type was used, handset one letter at a time, or lines of text

cast from a Linotype machine; and images were etched or engraved into metal plates. Nowadays, photopolymer plates are more often used. Polymer plates are created by a photographic method and are made from a thin polymer that is designed to be adhered to a printing base to make the relief image/form exactly 23.3172mm tall. They are relatively cheap to order from plate-making companies from image files supplied by the customer (see Suppliers).

If you are printing in a community shop, be sure to explain what type of project you will be printing and they can give you a recommendation of what type of press will be best suited for the job. Also ask them if they have a printing base to use polymer plates and what kind of base they have. If you are unsure of what kind of polymer plate to order, let the plate company know what kind of base you will be using and they can recommend the correct type.

Polymer plates hold very fine details, are strong enough to give a deep impression into the paper, and can be used for thousands of impressions if you keep them in good shape: always clean plates well after printing (I use Eco-House citrus cleaner) and store flat in a dark place in a plastic, zip-top bag. However, there are other ways to create an image to print on a letterpress. A popular option is to carve a lino block (see pages 58–67). Wood-mounted lino blocks, available at art supply stores, are usually close to letterpress height, and you can glue card stock or chipboard to the base to build them up to the necessary height. Many shops also have collections of metal type and vintage printers' cuts to print from.

MY INSPIRATIONS

Many things inspire me, from the natural world to cityscapes, and visiting natural history museums and fine art galleries is very important to me. Some of my favourite inspirations include: artists – Swoon, Kara Walker, Mazatl, Henry Darger, Lisa Solomon, Mikey Walsh; printing businesses – Starshaped Press, Banquet Workshop, Pistachio Press, Yellow Owl Workshop; and music – Leon Bridges, the Thermals, Billie Holiday, to name just three.

At Blackbird, we custom mix most of our print colours from quick-drying, rubber-based letterpress inks. This is our swatch board where we keep unused mixed inks in small envelopes that are labelled with an ink swatch, approximate recipe for the colour, and what greeting card the ink has been used for.

Camper ADVENTURE

Letterpress Print

The camper is the perfect metaphor for adventure. I have designed it as a flat card to be sent to the lucky recipient to cut out and assemble into a 3D model. It is a letterpress print in two colours. There's a camper template on page 126 to get you started, but I've left filling in the details and creating the scene accessories to your imagination. I hope you will apply my instructions to make more 3D models.

DRAWING PAPER • PENCIL • BLACK MARKER PEN • RULER • ERASER • COMPUTER AND SCANNER • ADOBE PHOTOSHOP, OR SIMILAR IMAGE SOFTWARE PROGRAM • PHOTOPOLYMER PLATES FOR PRINTING • ACCESS TO LETTERPRESS AND PRINTING BASE • MINIMUM 270gsm RECYCLED COVER PAPER • LETTERPRESS INK • PALETTE KNIFE • SOLVENTS FOR CLEANING • SCISSORS • CRAFT KNIFE • SCORING TOOL • GLUE

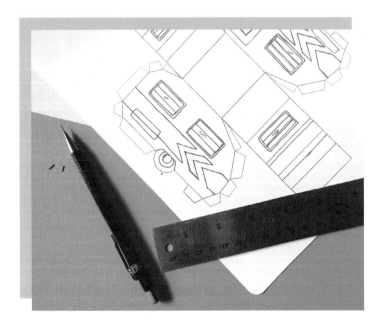

1 Draw the object you want to make in 2D. I start by drawing the shape and each side of the object with sides connected where appropriate, and then I add the 5mm construction tabs to use for gluing. (Alternatively, use the template on page 126.) Now fill in the details of your design. If you have used a pencil to draw your illustration, go over all lines (anything you want to print) with a black marker pen to make them as dark as possible. Mark the lines that will fold as dotted lines and the lines to be cut as solid lines. Erase the pencil marks. It often takes several drawings and tweaks to make a model that fits perfectly together.

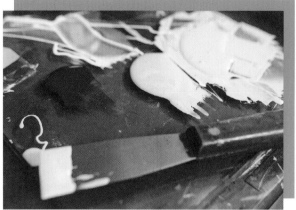

2 Once your drawing is complete, it is time to format it in preparation to make the printing plate. Scan your drawing at high resolution. Open in Photoshop or equivalent image software and format the drawing into a bitmap file, reducing all lines to just black and white. If designing the card to be two-colour, separate each colour into its own separate file. I used polymer plates to print this card (see Tools and Techniques for more information about polymer plates and ordering).

3 Choose the colour for the accent or lightest colour. Mix the combination of ink to create the right colour. With letterpress ink, if it is light, always start with white ink and add to that. Cut your paper down to the correct size, keeping in mind that the press you will print on may have a specific registration margin that needs to be added (this is an area that is needed to feed into the press but that does not print). My finished card measures 14.5cm x 22cm.

4 Now to prepare the printing set up. Lock the printing base in the press bed. Place the plate on the base. Ink up the press, print a proof, and adjust the registration of the paper and plate as needed. Print the first colour. Clean the press at the end of the first printing run.

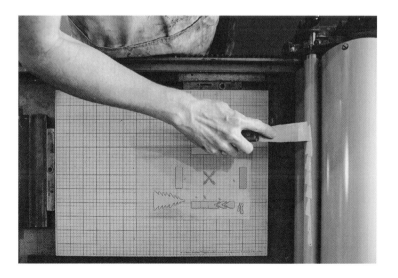

5 Mix the ink for the second colour. Place the second colour plate on the base. Ink up the press and adjust the registration of the paper and plate as needed.

6 Print the second colour. Clean the press at the end of the second printing run.

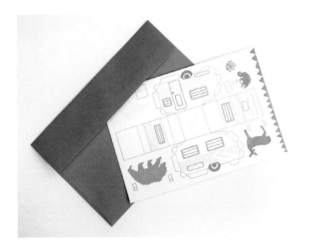

7 Admire your finished printed card. It is now ready to send as is, or you can assemble it and give it as a constructed model.

8 To construct the model, use scissors to cut out the camper along the solid line outline.

9 Use a craft knife to cut the tabs, and then use a scoring tool to score the fold lines. Fold and glue each tab in place, one at a time.

RIGHT The North Star Bear is letterpress printed in light grey and soft green on bamboo paper and then die-cut in our studio. We assemble the parts to create the bear novelty card. It measures approximately 12.5cm x 9.5cm and has four movable legs attached with two tiny brads. The design printed on the bear is inspired by the northern sky and constellations. Our planet is warming and this pays homage to the great animals that live among the ice.

BELOW The BFF card is based on our sweet dog, Jack, once a guard dog and now retired. His mouth is open to hold a gift card, note, paper bone, or money. The card is letterpress printed from an original illustration in a dark teal ink onto recycled paper and it measures approximately 9.5cm x 21cm. The BFF card has been photographed against a background of papercut grass.

CONTRIBUTORS

PROJECT CARD ARTISTS

Kirsty Elson
Website: kirstyelson.co.uk
Twitter: @KirstyElson
Instagram: @kirstyelson

Lucy Featherstone
Website: lucyfeatherstone.co.uk
Twitter: @FeatherLucy
Instagram: @lucy_featherstone

Lynn Giunta
Instagram: @lynn_giunta

Sarah Hamilton
Website: sarahhamiltonprints.com
Twitter: @SarahHamiltonPS
Instagram: @sarahhamiltonprints

Jessica Hogarth
Website: jessicahogarth.com
Twitter: @JessHogarth
Instagram: @jessicahogarth

Kathryn Hunter
Website: blackbirdletterpress.com
Website: kathrynhunterfineart.com
Twitter: @blackbirdletter
Instagram: @blackbirdletterpress

Anna Jackson
Website: blackcactuslondon.com
Twitter: @BlackCactus
Instagram: blackcactuslondon

Sam Marshall
Website: sammarshallart.com
Twitter: @sammarshallart
Instagram: @sammarshallart

Sarah Morpeth
Website: sarahmorpeth.com
Twitter: @skiptotheend
Instagram: @sarahmorpeth

Gabriela Szulman
Website: gabrielaszulman.com
Twitter: @gabrielaszulman
Instagram: @gabrielaszulman

OTHER CONTRIBUTORS

Jehane Boden Spiers
Website: yellowhouseartlicensing.com
Twitter: @yellowhouse_uk

Jakki Brown
Website: progressivegreetings.co.uk
Twitter: @PGLiveLondon

David Oakes
Website: drawings.davidoakes.co.uk
Twitter: @David_Oakes
Instagram: @doakesdoakes

The cards seen on page 4 (opposite the contents page) have been supplied with the kind permission of, from left to right:
Row 1 Sarah Morpeth, Jo Angell (joangell.com), Kate Broughton (katebroughton.co.uk)
Row 2 Lisa Jones (lisajonesstudio.com), Justine Ellis (justineellis.co.uk), Jane Ormes (janeormes.co.uk)
Row 3 Tara Dennis (seedprints.co.uk), Stuart Low (stuartlow.co.uk), Georgia Bosson (georgiabosson.co.uk)
Row 4 Sarah Raphael Balme (balhamcat.wixsite.com/raphael-balme), Kate Marsden (madebymrsm.co.uk)
Row 5 Kathryn Hunter, Sarah Hamilton, Justine Ellis, Rachel Stanners (pricklepress.co.uk)
Row 6 Sarah Hamilton, Kirsty Elson, Jill Meager (jillmeager.com), Sarah Cowen (lettica.co.uk)

The following cards on pages 6 and 22 have been included with the kind permission of the attributed artists:
Suns Rob Hodgson (robhodgson.com)
Koala Hannah Pontin (hannahpontin.com)
Partridge Harriet Russell (harrietrussell.co.uk)

SUPPLIERS

Listed below are the recommendations of some of our contributors' favourite suppliers. Many of these suppliers have a wide range of useful tools and materials.

BASIC TOOL KIT

Cowling and Wilcox
cowlingandwilcox.com
For art materials and tools.

Hobbycraft
hobbycraft.co.uk
For patterned papers and card, pens and art equipment.

Paperchase
paperchase.co.uk
For patterned papers, card and brightly coloured envelopes in a range of standard sizes.

The Bag N Box Man Ltd
bagnboxman.co.uk
For cello bags and packaging.

John Purcell Paper
johnpurcell.net
For art paper – their range and knowledge is second to none.

SILKSCREEN PRINTING

Handprinted
handprinted.net
For a wide range of printmaking equipment including silkscreens and sundries.

AP Fitzpatrick
shop.apfitzpatrick.co.uk
For top-quality screen-printing inks, base medium and stencil fluids.

COLLAGE

Dover Books
store.doverpublications.com
For royalty-free images.

New York Public Library Digital Image Collection
digitalcollections.nypl.org
For royalty-free images.

PAPERCUTTING

Jackson's Art Supplies
jacksonsart.com
For Fabriano cartridge paper.

EcoCraft
eco-craft.co.uk
For recycled coloured paper.

LINOCUT PRINTING

Intaglio Printmakers
intaglioprintmaker.com
For lino blocks.

Jackson's Art Supplies
jacksonsart.com
For inks.

DECOUPAGE

Hallmark Cards
hallmark.com
For tissue papers.

Dick Blick Art Materials
dickblick.com
For illustration board; Mod Podge; and matte or gloss medium.

HANDSTITCH ART

GF Smith
gfsmith.com
For paper.

Gutermann
guetermann.com
For threads, especially metallics.

DIGITAL ILLUSTRATION

Adobe
adobe.com
For free trial download and information on subscription.

TEXTILE FOILING

Art to Silkscreen
silkscreeningprintsupplies.co.uk
For screen-printing screens, squeegees, foils and adhesive.

Speedball
speedballart.com
For screen-printing screens and squeegees.

Applicraft
applicraft.co.uk
For foils and adhesive.

LETTERPRESS PRINTING

For a letterpress shared workspace:
letterpressalive.co.uk
londonprintstudio.org.uk
britishletterpress.co.uk

For photo polymer plates:
centuriongraphics.co.uk
rankingraphics.co.uk
lymebaypress.com

TEMPLATES

Out of This World

See page 88

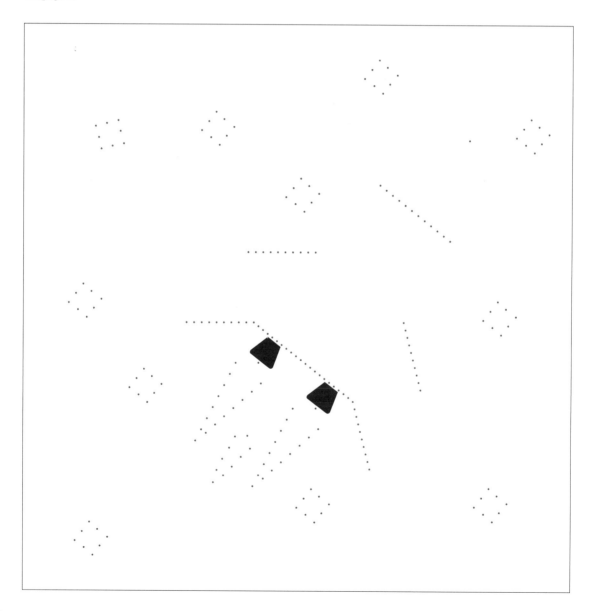

Camper Adventure

See page 116

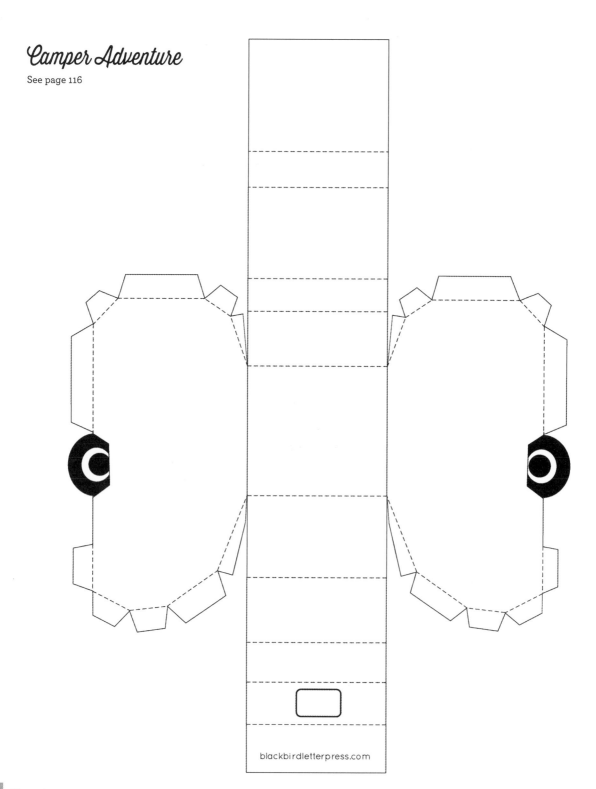

blackbirdletterpress.com

INDEX

Acknowledgements

In addition to the inspirational artists who have created the designs for the card projects, I'd like to say a huge 'Thank You' to the many talented artists who have allowed us to feature their cards. Thanks also go to Jakki, Jehane and David for contributing their insightful chapters.

I am indebted to all at Pavilion – Katie, Amy, Ione, Michelle and Sally – and also to project editor Cheryl Brown. It has been a privilege to learn from the best.

Special mention goes to Patricia van den Akker at the Design Trust (thedesigntrust.co.uk) and to *Mollie Makes* magazine for backing the 'Just a Card' campaign – both are true champions of artists, makers and creative businesses. Do meet our wonderful 'Just a Card' team at justacard.org and find out more about the campaign.

Love to Mark, Luke and Rossie.

And finally, I'm incredibly grateful to everyone who has supported my artwork over the years – thank you so much for helping me do what I love so much.

Picture Credits

All photography by Kristy Noble with the exception of the photographs on pages: 1, 2, 6/7 (James Balston); 11 (reproduced by kind permission of Jakki Brown); 12 (Sam Marshall); 17 (Gabriela Szulman); 20, 21, (images supplied by Yellow House Art Licensing); 22 (James Balston); 23 (Jessica Hogarth); 26/27, 30, 31 (James Balston); 32 (Fiona Murray); 33 top (Yeshen Venema); 34, 35, 36, 37 top, 38 (James Balston); 40–49 (Kevin Cozad, with styling by Nicole Cawlfield and art direction by Danielle Mousley); 52 top (Phil Gevaux); 60 top and 61 left (Rita Platts); 59, 61 right, 62–66 (Sam Marshall); 70 top (Helen Bottrill); 70 below (Kirsty Elson); 79 (Gabriela Szulman); 96 (Yeshen Venema); 97 (Jessica Hogarth); 112, 113, 114 below, 115–119 (Lindsey Smith); 114 top (Sadie Landry); 120 (Kathryn Hunter); 121 (Katherine Holly).

First published in the United Kingdom in 2017 by
Pavilion Books Company Limited
1 Gower Street
London
WC1E 6HD

ISBN 978-1-91090-457-2

A CIP catalogue record for this book is available from the British Library.

10 9 8 7 6 5 4 3 2 1

Reproduction by Mission
Printed and bound by Toppan Leefung Printing Ltd, China

This book can be ordered direct from the publisher at www.pavilionbooks.com